SCHUBERT

his life and times

Franz Peter Schubert (1797-1828), lithograph by Josef Teltscher

SCHUBERT

his life and times

Peggy Woodford

Paganiniana Publications, Inc.
211 West Sylvania Avenue, Neptune City, N.J. 07753

To my godson, Ben

ISBN 0-87666-640-3

Schubert: His Life and Times by Peggy Woodford was originally published in 1978 by Midas Books, 12 Dene Way, Speldhurst, Tunbridge Wells, Kent TN3 ONX England. Copyright © 1978 by Peggy Woodford, reprinted by permission of the publisher.

Expanded Edition of *Schubert: His Life and Times* © 1980 by Paganiniana Publications, Inc. A considerable amount of new material has been added to the original text, including but not limited to illustrations and their captions. Copyright is claimed for this new material.

Published by PAGANINIANA PUBLICATIONS, INC.
211 West Sylvania Avenue
Neptune City, New Jersey 07753

Contents

Acknowledgements

I would like to thank Richard and Katrina Burnett for their invaluable advice about Viennese fortepianos, Eric Sams for his guidance on Schubert's disease, Dame Janet Baker for her comment on the interpretation of Schubert's songs and Peter Southwell-Sander and Charles Baty for their careful checking of my original manuscript.

Selected Bibliography

Abraham, Gerald — Schubert. A Symposium. London 1952.

Barea, Ilsa — Vienna, Legend and Reality. London 1966.

Barthold, Kenneth van — The Story of the Piano. London 1975.

Brown, Maurice J. E. — Schubert. A Critical Biography. London 1958
    — Essays on Schubert. London 1966.

Capell, Richard — Schubert's Songs. London 2nd Ed. 1957.

Deutsch, Otto Erich — Schubert: A Documentary Biography. London 1946.
    — Schubert. Memoirs by his friends. London 1958.
    — Thematic Catalogue of Schubert's Works. London 1951.

Einstein, Alfred — Schubert. London 1951.

Fischer-Dieskau, Dietrich — A Biographical Study of Schubert's Songs. London 1976.

Flower, Newman — Franz Schubert, the Man and his Circle. London 1928.

Hutchings, Arthur — Schubert (Master Musician Series). London 1973.

Prawer, S. S. (Editor and Translator) — Penguin Book of Lieder. London 1964.

Reed, John — The Final Years. London 1972.

Oxford History of Music, Vol. 5: 'The Viennese Period'.

Chapter 1

First Years

'This child will become a master such as few have been.' — Dr Anton Schmidt, reported by Josef Spaun

Schubert's story is one of the most touching of all composers; he died young, aged only thirty-one, and left a larger number of works than any other great composer; he died with his genius unrecognised, except by his friends, and it took most of the nineteenth century for his true stature to be realized. Now, 150 years after his death, we find it hard to believe that any man so gifted could have had so little success within his own lifetime. In 1827, a year before Schubert died, an Englishman, Edward Holmes, visited Vienna and wrote an account of the state of music in this centre of music; he never once mentions Schubert's name. In 1830 a French scholar, M. Fetis, and in 1833 the music historian, Raphael Georg Kiesewetter, described the Viennese musical scene without making any reference to Schubert. This complete obscurity was an astonishing phenomenon: after all, Schubert was not a recluse, some of his works were both published and performed in Austria, and his many friends were of the Viennese intelligentsia. No other composer has had such an extended posthumous rise from obscurity to fame. Schubert once said to his lifelong friend, Josef von Spaun: 'Secretly, in my heart of hearts, I still hope to make something of myself, but who can do anything after Beethoven?' A year after Schubert's death, Spaun himself wrote 'In spite of all the admiration I have felt for my dear friend . . . we shall never make a Mozart or a Haydn out of him . . .'

* * *

Franz Peter Schubert was born on 31 January 1797 in an alcove in his parents' crowded apartment in the Viennese suburb of Himmelpfortgrund. Schubert's father, Franz Theodor (1763-1830) was a farmer's son from Moravia; his mother, Elisabeth Vietz (1756-1812) was a master locksmith's daughter from Silesia. They met and married in Vienna, where Franz Theodor was working for

his brother Karl as an assistant schoolmaster. Their first child,
Ignaz, was born in 1785, two months after their wedding; thirteen
more children followed in the space of sixteen years. Only Ignaz,
Ferdinand (the tenth child, born in 1794), Franz Karl (1785), Franz
Peter (the twelfth child), and Maria Theresia, the fourteenth child
born in 1801 when Elisabeth Schubert was 45, survived.

The house in which Schubert was born, now 54 Nussdorfer-
strasse, contained sixteen apartments each comprising one large
room and a kitchen. The Schubert family rented two of these, and
in the same rooms during the day Franz Theodor taught his
elementary school of several classes. These overcrowded conditions
were normal in Vienna then; in the nine streets of the Himmelpfortgrund suburb there were 86 houses holding more than 3,000
inhabitants. The population of the inner city of Vienna was then
about 50,000; the total population including the suburbs was something under 300,000. The Schuberts' living conditions were
unusual only in that during the day 200 boys crowded into the
apartment. Franz Theodor was obviously a successful schoolmaster, because as numbers increased he had to give two sessions a
day, with 100 boys at a time. As soon as his own sons were old
enough, they were persuaded to become his assistant teachers.

In 1801 Franz Theodor bought and moved into bigger premises
in a nearby side street, the Säulengasse. Here the school continued
to expand and flourish, and young Schubert received a thorough
basic education. His father was a good teacher, and recognized early
that his son Franz Peter was exceptional. These early years have
been described by Ferdinand:

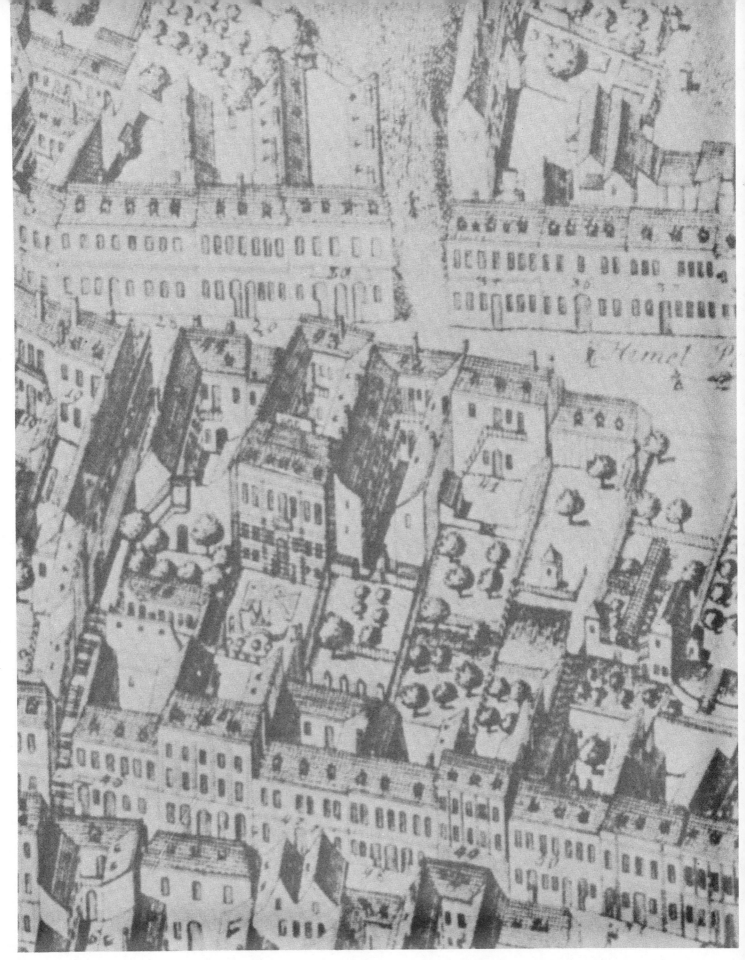

Schubert's birthplace, at foot of street leading to top of picture

The Liechtental parish church of Schubert's youth

Modern view of the area, showing the Liechtental church

In Franz his father, who earlier had given their first lessons in violin playing also to Ignaz and Ferdinand, and afterwards to Franz himself, perceived great talent for music from early childhood. Dear, good Franz now received lessons in pianoforte playing from his brother Ignaz. Later he was taught violin and pianoforte playing, as well as singing, by the choirmaster Michael Holzer, who several times asserted with tears in his eyes that he had never yet had such a pupil: 'For,' said he, 'whenever I wished to impart something new to him, he always knew it already. I often looked at him in silent wonder.'

Schubert was then some 10 years old, and in his 11th year he was a first soprano in the Liechtental church. Already at that time he delivered everything with the most appropriate expression; in those days he also played a violin solo in the organ-loft of the church and already composed small songs, string quartets and pianoforte pieces.

It is not surprising that Spaun described this start as 'a musical education rare for his tender age'.

The first important turning point in Schubert's life came in 1808, when the best educational institution in the city of Vienna, the Imperial and Royal Seminary, advertised in May for two boy choristers to sing in the Imperial and Royal Court Chapel, and be educated in the grammar school attached to the seminary. Ferdinand describes his brother's audition:

In October 1808 our Schubert was thus presented to the Imperial Seminary Directorate and had to sing for his trial. The boy wore a light

Courtyard of Schubert's birthplace facing the garden (*Schubert Museum*)

blue, whitish coat, so that the other people, including the remaining children who were also to be admitted to the Seminary, made fun of him among themselves with such remarks as 'That is doubtless a miller's son; he won't fail', etc. However, the schoolmaster's son made a sensation, not only by his white frock coat but also with the Court musical Directors, Salieri and Eybler and with the singing-Master Körner, as well as by his certainty in sight-reading the trial song submitted to him. He was accordingly admitted.

(Millers always wore white, as did the miller in Schubert's own song cycle, *Die Schöne Müllerin*.)

Even allowing for a proud brother's natural exaggeration in Ferdinand's memoirs, it still seems clear that Schubert's talent was recognized early. Antonio Salieri was a most important man; a former enemy of Mozart's, he had dominated the musical scene in Vienna for forty years. His approval of Schubert must have been a great encouragement.

The education offered at the Seminary was first that of an excellent preparatory choir school; and then, when the boys' voices broke, if their 'morals and studies' were good enough, they could stay on for a full grammar-school education. Even as early as Schubert's first term in the new year of 1809, it is clear from surviving school reports that his academic ability was of a high order. His studies included Latin, mathematics, natural history and physics, geography and history, and religious instruction. He was receiving the best education available and his fellow schoolboys were of a high calibre. Thus, early on, he mixed with his intellectual peers.

But it was the musical life at the Seminary which was so essential to Schubert's growth as a composer. He was taught piano and organ by Wenzel Ruzicka, a professional organist who also taught the viola and cello; Ruzicka is reported to have said of Schubert's musical talent: 'This one's learnt it from God'. Violin and singing were also taught and the Seminary had a flourishing orchestra which played a symphony and one or two overtures every evening. Schubert played first violin, and people gathered in the square outside the Seminary to listen to the music pouring through the open windows.

Several of Schubert's friends at the Seminary described their schooldays together; Anton Holzapfel wrote of Schubert, who was five years his junior:—

When I got to know him well he was in the fourth grammar class, a short, stocky figure of a boy with a friendly round face and strongly marked features. . . even in those days his intellectual activity was far in advance of

Antonio Salieri (1750-1825), admirer of Gluck, rival of Mozart, teacher of Beethoven, Schubert and Liszt. Anonymous oil painting (Gesellschaft der Musikfreunde, Vienna)

Vienna: St. Stephen's Cathedral from the Rothenturmstrasse (*from a watercolour by R. Alt*)

his years; this was proved by a long poem of his, dating from that time, which I kept but which has since been lost, written in the lively style of Klopstock's odes, a style hardly understood by us pupils, and on the theme, incidentally, of God's omnipotence . . .

As well as this interesting insight into Schubert's adolescent development, Holzapfel has left us a vivid description of the Seminary orchestra. Schubert was apparently the 'orchestral assistant';

this very irksome job of looking after the stringing of the instruments, lighting the tallow candles, putting out the parts, and keeping the instruments and scores in good condition was filled for many years by Franz Schubert who, at the same time, also took part every day as a violinist. In addition to this daily practice and the church performances of the choirboy scholars, little groups . . . were formed for the performance of string and vocal quartets; songs at the fortepiano, especially the ballads and songs of Zumsteeg, also became very popular with us. Altogether there was a relatively serious musical endeavour among us at the time, in which in his early days Schubert already took a most active part . . . year in, year out, at

11

The Vienna Boys' Choir,
originally the Choir of
the Hofkapelle (Court
Chapel) which was
founded by the Emperor
Maximilian I, had both
Haydn and Schubert as
members in their
youthful years (*Photo: M.
Hürlimann*)

our daily performances all the symphonies by Josef Haydn and Mozart, the first two symphonies of Beethoven, as well as all the overtures we could tackle at that time ... were regularly performed, and we also played through the greater part of the classical quartets of Haydn and Mozart; everything, of course, extremely roughly and inaccurately and on bad instruments ...

Although this was all written down long afterwards in 1858, it has a directness about it which hints that Holzapfel is remembering accurately.

Thus Schubert could not have had a more thorough grounding in music, and was familiar not only with the great composers, but with the fashionable mediocrities. Spaun remembers how he disliked Kenner's symphonies, then much in vogue:

Schubert was annoyed whenever one of them was played and used to say repeatedly, during the performance, 'Oh, how boring'. He did not understand how one could perform such stuff, as he calls it, when Haydn had written symphonies without number.

12

Schubert met Josef von Spaun (1788-1865), who was to be his most loyal, generous and sensitive friend, at the Seminary, where Spaun was studying law. Although eleven years older, he noticed the young Franz at once.

I took my place as leader of the second violins and the little Schubert played from the same music, standing behind me. Very soon I became aware that the little musician far surpassed me in the sureness of his beat. My attention having been drawn to him by this, I noticed how the otherwise quiet and indifferent looking boy surrendered himself in the most lively way to the impressions of the beautiful symphony we were playing.

Spaun was promptly drawn to this talented boy, and once found him in a music room alone, playing a Mozart sonata.

At my request and aware of my sympathy, he played me a minuet of his own invention. He was shy about it, and blushed, but my approval pleased him. He told me that secretly he often wrote down his thoughts in music, but his father must not know about it, as he was dead against his devoting himself to music. After that I used to slip manuscript paper into his hands from time to time.

Franz Schubert senior,
father of the composer

This is the first intimation of the friction that existed between father and son: Franz Theodor, though delighted with his son's musical talent, wanted him to receive the excellent all-round education offered by the Seminary in order to become a schoolmaster. Schubert for the time being acquiesced from lack of alternatives, but always gave far more time to music than his father ever suspected. In consequence his academic work suffered. Franz Theodor was a conservative, rigidly religious man, strict but warm-hearted; there is no evidence that the friction, despite occasional rows, ever developed into bitter conflict. Both seemed to have been tolerant at heart of each other's very different personalities. Schubert's mother Elisabeth, described as a quiet, much loved person, remains a shadow; perhaps he inherited his sense of humour and lightness of touch from her, but she left behind nothing to show what she was really like. And in May, 1812, when Schubert was fifteen, she died.

The disease which killed her was typhus abdominalis, the very same disease of which her composer son would die. Again, there are no contemporary documents to tell us how he was affected by his mother's death. Ten years later he wrote an allegorical story called 'My Dream' which describes a mother's death and the tears that followed. Although this allegory is a typical effusion of German romanticism and not to be taken as autobiographical, the underlying sense of grief can be felt.

The Seminary (*the building on the left*) as it was in Schubert's time, with the old University which has since been demolished

Very soon after this family tragedy, Schubert's life at the Seminary took a new turn: he began to take counterpoint lessons with Salieri. This was a special privilege, because Salieri did not usually teach mere Seminary boys. It appears his interest in Schubert was aroused when he was shown a song the boy had composed, *Hagars Klage* (Hagar's Lament), an ambitious and lengthy ballad-like work written the year before, in March 1811, and the first of Schubert's songs to survive. It is an assured and mature work for a fourteen-year-old, and tells of a mother's lament for her dying child — a painfully familiar theme in Schubert's own family life. The poem had already been set by Johann Zumsteeg, considered one of the best song writers of his day. Schubert loved, admired and was inspired by his songs, and this enthusiasm as well as natural aptitude had led him early into composing songs himself.

What Salieri, a champion of the Italian style, taught Schubert is not clear. Holzapfel says:

I recall clearly that this instruction was but very scanty . . . and that, on the whole, it consisted only in the superficial correction of small exercises in part writing, though most of it, and this may have been the most successful part, consisted in the reading and playing of scores. At the beginning Schubert was obliged, first and foremost, to work through a large number of extremely dull old Italian scores and it was only later that he went through the whole of Gluck, from whose works Schubert often played things to us, which I still remember . . .

Holzapfel knew Schubert well at this stage in their lives, and was taken several times into Schubert's home. He says that Schubert's father 'did not welcome visits from his seminary friends . . .

Christoph Willibald
Gluck (1714-1787):
terracotta bust at the
Royal College of Music,
London

An early silhouette of
Schubert during his time
at the Seminary

because of the economic situation at home' — the pressures of teaching and lack of money.

Written in Schubert's hand at the end of a manuscript of part of a Mass in the Court Chapel, are to be seen the words: 'Schubert, Franz, crowed for the last time, 26th July 1812'. Now that his voice had broken, he could have been asked to leave the Seminary; but his grades were still all good or very good in every part of his report, and so his continued education there was assured. Though he is reported by Spaun to have called the Seminary a 'prison', he appears to have been adequately happy, mainly because he had so much time and opportunity to give to his music. The first letter of Schubert's to survive also dates from this period; its lively turn of phrase suddenly presents Franz Peter Schubert to us full face as a high-spirited, witty and normal schoolboy:

24th November 1812

Straight out with what troubles me, and so I shall come to my purpose the sooner, and you will not be detained by any precious beating about the bush. I have long been thinking about my situation and found that, although it is satisfactory on the whole, it is not beyond some improvement here and there. You know from experience that we all like to eat a roll or a few apples sometimes, the more so if after a middling lunch one may not look for a miserable evening meal for eight and a half hours. This wish, which has often become insistent, is now becoming more and more frequent, and I had willy-nilly to make a change. The few groats I receive from Father go to the deuce the very first days, and what am I to do for the rest of the time; 'Whosoever believeth on Him shall not be put to shame.' Matthew, iii. 4. I thought so too. — How if you were to let me have a few Kreuzer a month? You would not so much as know it, while I in my cell should think myself lucky, and be content. I repeat, I lean upon the words of the Apostle Matthew, where he says: 'He that hath two coats, let him give one to the poor,' &c. Meanwhile I hope that you will give ear to the voice that calls unceasingly to you to remember

Your
Loving, poor, hopeful
and again poor brother
Franz.

The Biblical quotations, perhaps a flippant aping of his father, are given the wrong sources, probably on purpose.

There are several descriptions of Schubert at this age, but the most precise and vivid description is by Georg Franz Eckel, another Seminary friend who was asked in 1858 to write down all he remembered of his young contemporary. Before beginning his detailed description Eckel points out that though he never saw Schubert again after he left the Seminary, his image 'remains

15

vividly in my memory despite the forty-five years that have passed since then'. Eckel became a doctor of medicine and perhaps this is one reason why his description has a physiological exactitude which accords with later portraits of Schubert.

The figure small but stocky, with strongly developed, firm bones and firm muscles, rounded rather than angular. Neck short and powerful; shoulders, chest and pelvis broad and finely arched; arms and thighs rounded; hands and feet small; his walk brisk and vigorous. His head, which was rather large, round and strongly built, was surrounded by a shock of brown curly hair. His face, in which the forehead and chin were predominant, showed features which were not really handsome so much as expressive and strong. His eyes, which were soft and, if I am not mistaken, light brown in colour and which burned brightly when he was excited, were heavily overshadowed by rather prominant orbital ridges and bushy eyebrows; because of this, and because of frequent screwing-up of his eyelids, as habitually happens with short-sighted people, they appeared smaller than they really were. Nose medium-size, blunt, rather turned-up and connected by a soft inward curve to the full, well-developed, tightly shutting and usually closed lips. On his chin the so-called beauty dimple. His complexion pale but bright, as with all men of genius. The lively play of his features, giving expression to the constant inner excitement, proclaimed sometimes, in the deeply furrowed forehead and the tightly-closed lips, the serious, and sometimes, in the soft light in his eye and the smiling mouth, the charming images of his creative genius.

(Schubert's eyes were variously described as grey or brown; accounts differ, and since he wore glasses most of the time they might have obscured the colour, which was clearly a mixture of both.) Eckel says that Schubert was lively, 'though more in manner than in words, which were mostly short and to the point and revealed a good measure of humour'. This was a characteristic that did not change; however much time he spent with his boisterous, talkative companions he did not waste words. His humour, his genius and his quiet strength of character made him a central figure in his wide and changing circle of friends who were an essential part of his existence, from his days at the Seminary until his early death.

By 1813, Schubert was neglecting his other subjects for music to such a degree that his grades dropped markedly and his place at the Seminary was in jeopardy. In a document signed by the Emperor Franz I, himself, it was decided that Schubert could stay on provided his work regained its former excellent standard. The document dated October 1813 stated:

singing and music are but a subsidiary matter, while good morals and diligence in study are of prime importance and an indispensable duty for all those who wish to enjoy the advantages of an Endowment.

Drawing of a student, probably Schubert, by Moritz von Schwind

Pencil sketch of Schubert, found in family album of Moritz von Schwind

Emperor Franz I in the uniform of a Field-Marshal (*from an oil painting by Friedrich von Amerling*)

Schubert's endowment paid his fees; without it he could not stay at the Seminary. By the end of November, for reasons which are not clear, Schubert had resigned this endowment and left the Seminary. He obviously could not accept the Emperor's dictum that music was a 'subsidiary matter'; his friend Spaun described how he used all his school time for music.

He composed extraordinarily quickly and the preparation periods he used uninterruptedly for composing, as a result of which, of course, the school came off badly. His father, otherwise a very good man, discovered the cause of his backwardness in his work and there was a tremendous row and further prohibition . . .

So at the end of 1813 Schubert, now nearly seventeen years old, returned to live with his family. The situation at home was radically changed, because Franz Theodor had remarried six months before and his new wife Anna, a silk merchant's daughter,

17

was only fourteen years older than Schubert himself and from the start was a good friend to him. Her presence in the crowded apartment must have eased the tensions between father and son. Franz Theodor was determined that his musical son should become a schoolmaster like his brothers; he made arrangements for Schubert to attend teacher training college, which he did for the academic year 1813-14.

But he kept in close contact with his friends, and Spaun in particular. Spaun describes how during the various holidays he

Vienna: the Michaelplatz and Burgtheater *(from an anonymous coloured engraving)*

Theodor Körner

took Schubert to the opera, where they sat in the cheapest seats losing themselves in Mozart's *Die Zauberflöte*, Cherubini's *Medea*, Gluck's *Iphigénie en Tauride* and many others. Spaun tells a story about the visit to *Iphigénie* which illustrates the unexpectedly fiery and passionate side to Schubert's character. While Spaun, Schubert and a poet friend, Theodor Körner, were having supper together and 'revelling loudly in the enjoyment of what we had heard, a University professor at the next table made fun of our enthusiasm' and criticised the singing.

Our fury over these impudent remarks knew no bounds — Körner and Schubert sprang up in a rage and, in doing so, the latter knocked over his glass, which was full of beer, and there was the most violent exchange of words which, because of the opponent's obstinacy, would have turned to blows if some calming voices, which came in on our side, had not appeased us. (Schubert was ablaze with anger over this, a state which otherwise was quite foreign to his gentle disposition.)

Schubert always hated pretentiousness of any sort and was impatient of unnecessary ignorance and ineptitude. This impatience above all made him temperamentally unsuited to be a schoolmaster, a profession he had no love for whatever.

Chapter 2

The Imperial City

'This Vienna, with all its memories of the greatest German masters, must be fruitful ground for the musician's fancy.' — Robert Schumann

During Schubert's childhood and adolescence, Vienna had undergone several political and military upheavals which made life stressful and unpleasant. Since 1792, when Franz I (1768-1835) was crowned German Emperor, Austria had been involved in wars with revolutionary France; there were short periods of costly peace, but the main picture is of wars against the marauding French under Napoleon Bonaparte which continued until his final defeat at Waterloo in 1815. Napoleon occupied Vienna twice; in 1805 and in 1809. Schubert had only just joined the Seminary in 1809, and his friend Spaun has left a description of the approach of the French army. Although the Seminary boys were forbidden to join the student corps, they did so and marched out enthusiastically.

On the third day, however, there came a supreme command from the Archduke Rainer, which made it our duty to resign at once; and as we were locked up in the Seminary for several days, there was an end to playing at soldiers for us.

Spaun goes on:

On the evening of 12 May, at 9 o'clock, the bombardment of the city began. It was a magnificent sight to see the glowing cannon-balls curving across the night sky, while the many conflagrations reddened the sky. Before our very eyes a ball from a howitzer fell in the University square and burst in one of the lovely fountains there; but all of a sudden there was a crash in the house itself, a howitzer shell having fallen on the Seminary building. It penetrated every floor down to the first and burst on the first floor in Prefect Walch's room, who was just turning the key to go in. It was a great stroke of luck that, on all three floors, the prefects happened not to be in their rooms, otherwise all three might have been killed.

They were just boys, full of the excitement of war; for patriotic adults life in Vienna could be very unpleasant, with the chronic

The French bombardment of Vienna on the night of 11-12 May 1809 (Österreichische National-bibliothek, Vienna)

Joseph von Spaun (*from an oil painting by Kupelwieser*)

shortages, inflation (prices trebled in four months) and sapped morale of an occupied city. The great contemporary poet Franz Grillparzer describes what it was like for a sensitive middle-class citizen, his father:

Then came the war events of 1809, the lost battles, the bombardment of the town, the entry of the French in Vienna, the paralysis of business, the billeting, the war tax and contributions; above all his patriotic heart was suffering torment under all these humiliations ... While expenses continued to mount with the rising prices, incomes gradually fell to an insignificant amount, until in the last months the entry he made in the ledger, with an uncertain hand, was *Nihil*. He even had to take up a loan,

21

Franz Grillparzer (1791-1872) a distinguished Austrian poet who delivered Beethoven's funeral oration and many of whose poems were set to music by Schubert. He was a close friend of the Fröhlich sisters

he, to whom the terms contractor of debts and thief were synonymous. To know that the town was occupied by the enemy was abominable to him, and to see a Frenchman was like a knife-thrust . . .

Grillparzer's reaction is different, and perhaps reflects that of many other young men like him:

I myself was no less an enemy of the French than my father, and yet Napoleon fascinated me with a magic power. I had hatred in my heart, I had never been addicted to military displays, and yet I missed not one of his reviews of troops at Schönbrunn and on the parade ground of the so-called Schmelz. I still see him before me, running rather than walking down the open-air steps of Schönbrunn, behind him the Crown Princes of Bavaria and Württemberg as aides-de-camp, and then standing there cast-iron, hands folded behind his back, to survey his hosts on their march past with the unmoved look of the lord and master.

In 1810 Napoleon married Emperor Franz's daughter Marie Louise and became Austria's ally. Only temporarily: in 1813 Austria united with Prussia and Russia and the three allied armies defeated Napoleon at Leipzig in October 1813. After his final defeat, the impressive Congress of Vienna took place between September 1814 and June 1815: it restored all possessions to her, so that her Empire now comprised Austria-Hungary with Venetia, Milan and other North Italian territories.

Thus from 1815 onwards for thirty years the Austrian Empire was outwardly settled but inwardly uneasy. The unease was caused partly by the way Franz I and his councillor, Prince Metternich, ran the country. O. E. Deutsch has described the Emperor as 'a domestic tyrant to the family of his people, thinking and taking care of everything, but in a petty way; much concerned about the loyalty of his subjects and ruthless in his persecution of elements dangerous to the throne.' This ruthlessness was endorsed by Prince Metternich, who helped to introduce a police state in Austria: from 1819, when Schubert and his friends were at a very vulnerable stage of their young adult lives, there was tough official censorship of books, words and music, newspapers etc; there was police surveillance of universities and prohibitions of such associations where the

The Grosse Galerie of Schönbrunn (*Photo: M. Hürlimann*)

A street scene in Vienna, with fruit and sweetmeat stalls, at the time of Schubert's youth

young intelligentsia could meet and plan, in Metternich's eyes, sedition. Young men met instead in the inns and coffee-houses which abounded in Vienna.

Only once did the police state bite viciously into Schubert's own circle. One of Schubert's early friends, the Tyrolese poet Johann Senn (1795-1857) was arrested in 1820 for suspected revolutionary activities; his rooms were searched one night and he, Schubert and three others, were arrested. All except Senn were released next morning after questioning; but Senn himself remained in detention for fourteen months and was then deported in exile to the Tyrol, his career ruined. He never saw Schubert again. When asked for his memories of Schubert he wrote in 1849:

The German struggles for liberation, from 1813 to 1815, had left in their wake a significant spiritual upheaval in Austria too. Among other things, there was gathered in Vienna at that time, as it were by instinct and not as the result of any intention, a splendid, companionable circle of young writers, poets, artists and cultured people generally, such as the Imperial city had scarcely ever seen hitherto and which, after it was disbanded, sowed seeds for the future in every direction.

Often a period of oppression has a stimulating effect on human society and endeavour, and this was clearly true of Schubert's young circle. But in the main the Viennese reaction was a different one. After such a long period of unrest and war, they wanted a cosy — *gemütlich* — safe and ordinary life, well-run and low-key. What is now known as the Biedermeier era (so called after a humorous imaginary character, Gottlieb Biedermeier, in a popular family magazine) had begun in earnest.

'Biedermeier' stood for a complete antipathy, born of the French Revolution and the Napoleonic Wars, to many of the ideals, standards and achievements of the eighteenth century. For by 1810 people were growing tired of living in an atmosphere of ferment and uncertainty, and craved domestic peace and stability, undoubted virtues in their way, but wholly incompatible with a society active in the speculation and experiment which beget great art. 'Biedermeier' was psychologically founded on a simplification of classical forms, a retreat from romantic pathos, and a devotion to sentimental lyricism. It lacked all symbolism, it was unimaginative, it knew not vague searchings, but clung solidly to the actual present, and above all to middle-class respectability.

(A. Hyatt King, in *A Schubert Symposium*)

Corpus Christe morning: a typical painting in the Wiener Biedermeier style, by Ferdinand Waldmüller

An amateur watercolour of the Biedermeier period, dating from about 1820, which is the first pictorial evidence we have of a tree forming the focal point in Christmas decorations in a Viennese home. This practice very quickly spread to England where it was fostered by the example set by Prince Albert

A pleasant, attractive, small-scale style flourished in the applied arts; life was well-polished, jolly but proper, sentimental but not passionate.

The Historical Museum of Vienna possesses a small album of prints and watercolours which are pure Biedermeier. By Franz von Paumgartten, they depict intimately and directly the life of a prosperous middle-class Viennese family in 1820. Schubert and his friends passed their lives against backgrounds like these; only when Schubert was at home with his family did he move in a world closer to working class poverty. The Paumgartten drawings show the air of friendly gaiety, of cosy home entertainment, so typical of Viennese society. Under one picture is written:

Love, friendship, concord, wit and pleasantry
Gladden each heart in this delightful company.

Market place in the courtyard of the Jesuit church dedicated to the Nine Choirs of Angels, Vienna

The inn at Galitzinberg
— a popular meeting
place for those on
excursions from Vienna

These people sang part songs together, and danced endlessly: the
waltz, the cotillon, the écossaise, the Ländler, the galop.

The Viennese lived lives full of music; no other European city
has ever had the musical pre-eminence that was Vienna's between
1770 and 1830. Mozart died there in 1791; Josef Haydn lived on
into Schubert's life for twelve years, and Beethoven absolutely
dominated the musical scene until his death in 1827. Vienna was a
centre of music publishing, and a centre of opera: there were five
theatres in those days, four of which concentrated on various types
of opera. The main one, the Kärntnertor Theatre, was devoted
mainly to Italian opera. There was music daily in the inns, particularly those in the suburbs and near the *Wienerwald* — the attractive
Vienna Woods; there were harp players on the Prater, organ
grinders in the streets, musical boxes and clocks in coffee houses.

The Emperor Franz was not an enthusiastic patron of music, but
he encouraged it: the *Gemütlichkeit* of home-music-making was
greatly preferable to revolutionary ardour. Every family had its
fortepiano; and many, like the Schuberts, played stringed instruments and performed quartets together. In 1814 the middle-class
Philharmonic Society — the *Gesellschaft der Musikfreunde* — was
founded and professional musicians were invited to give concerts to
large audiences. On a smaller scale, there were many *salons* where
music was performed to a very high standard; and there were small

string orchestras who played light music, serenades, dances etc for balls and gatherings. Every aspect of music-making, from the brass military band to the grand symphony, was to be found in Vienna. Almost everyone could read music and play some musical instrument; the whole of Vienna depended on music, on singing and dancing for its entertainment. With its immediacy and pungency, the sound of live music was everywhere. Schubert and his friends, like the rest of Vienna, were addicts of music, and particularly of the part-song and the dance. As M. J. E. Brown says in his biography of Schubert:

If we look at the composer against this background and try to see how it pervaded his thought and creative processes and what the music was which he poured out in response to its stimulus, the first thing that strikes us is this: he redeemed its triviality. He lent the inarticulate moods and desires of Vienna a voice — and through him they speak enduring things.

Bandstand in the courtyard of the Leopoldstadt inn, Vienna (1820)

28

Chapter 3

The Schoolmaster

'As for my feelings, I shall never be calculating and politic: I come straight out with what is in me, and that's that.' — Schubert

In the year after Schubert's death, his father wrote a very brief biographical note about him in which he said: 'Even in his earliest youth he loved society and he was never happier than when he could spend his leisure hours in the company of cheerful friends.'

In the two years after he left the Seminary, Schubert's friends were critically important. They drew him into the intellectual centre of avant-garde Vienna; poets, painters, actors and writers, lawyers and civil servants, all men of liberated and inquiring minds, became his close friends and their interest and enthusiasm encouraged him to devote his life increasingly to music.

The most important of these friends, of course, was Josef von Spaun who came from Linz in Upper Austria to Vienna in 1805. While Schubert was struggling, against his natural inclinations, to be a teacher, Spaun continued to see him frequently. Neither the fact that their backgrounds were very different — teaching children was considered a very humble occupation — nor the large age-gap between them deterred Spaun.

The words of no fewer than 47 of Schubert's songs were written by his friend Johann Mayrhofer

During this period I introduced him to my closest friends. First and foremost to the poet Johann Mayrhofer, my countryman and oldest friend. He had an exceptionally good ear and a great love for music. When Mayrhofer had heard some of Schubert's songs, he reproached me for having been much too modest in my praise of Schubert's talent. Mayrhofer sang and whistled Schubert's melodies the whole day long and poet and composer were soon the best of friends . . .

Mayrhofer's poems inspired Schubert to glorious songs, which are probably among his most beautiful works. Mayrhofer often maintained that he only liked and valued his poems after Schubert had set them to music.

Mayrhofer (1787-1836), from the beautiful town of Steyr in Upper Austria, was also a law student, although writing poetry was his passion. He was a moody introspective man, who eventually

A portrait of Franz Schober by Leopold Kupelwieser, painted in 1823. In the background can be seen Schober's birthplace Troup Castle near Mälmo in Sweden (*Schubert Museum*)

committed suicide as a result of chronic hypochondria. Schubert set a poem of his, *Am See* (On the Lake), Spaun then introduced them, and the beauty of the setting so delighted Mayrhofer that a very fruitful relationship began. Schubert was in time to set more of Mayrhofer's poems than those of any poet save Goethe. Mayrhofer was under no illusion how important these settings were: 'I wrote poetry, he composed what I had written, much of which owes its existence, its development and its popularity to his melodies . . .'

Spaun introduced many other men to his shy, amiable, brilliant friend of seventeen who lived in that depressing school in the Himmelpfortgrund, and foremost among them was Franz Schober who became, of all his circle, the one Schubert loved best. Schober (1796-1882) was born in Sweden of German/Austrian parents; he was a spasmodically wealthy dilettante who during his long life had many professions: writer, actor, painter and draughtsman, civil administrator. He was a charming but unstable aesthete whose stimulating and unorthodox approach to life appealed to Schubert strongly, from the very start of their acquaintance. He was irreligious, amoral, frequently indolent and frivolous, but in him Schubert, often to the disapproval of other more proper friends, found a soulmate. They referred to themselves as 'Schobert'. To Schubert's father Schober can only have been anathema.

As soon as he had finished training at St Anna's College he plunged straight into the daily grind at his father's school, but despite his busy life as a schoolmaster and his increasing circle of friends, Schubert found time to compose a great deal. His ability to work when surrounded by noise and distraction developed early and never left him. A friend at the Seminary, Albert Stadler, wrote:

It was interesting to see him compose. He very seldom made use of the pianoforte while doing it. He often used to say it would make him lose his train of thought. Quite quietly, and hardly disturbed by the unavoidable

Portrait believed to be that of Schubert at the age of 16

31

chatter and din of his friends around him, he would sit at the little writing-table, bent over the music paper and the book of poems (he was short-sighted), bite his pen, drum with his fingers at the same time, trying things out, and continue to write easily and fluently, without many corrections, as if it had to be like that and not otherwise.

By the end of 1814, Schubert's compositions were numerous: apart from what has not survived, he had written his first symphony in D, six string quartets for use in his family circle, and a considerable amount of church music (so delighted was Franz Theodor with a Mass of his son's that he gave him a Graf forte-piano, amongst the best to be had). An early octet for wind instruments has a comic childish inscription on it: 'Composed by Franz Schubert, Chapel Master to The Imperial Chappppelll at Nanking etc . . .' There are many minuets and dances both for orchestra and piano, two piano fantasias in C minor, one for solo piano and one for duet, piano sonatas, several overtures, and an operetta in three acts called *Des Teufels Lustschloss* (The Devil's Pleasaunce) and lastly, over fifty part songs and songs. It is amongst these songs that we first hear Schubert's authentic genius; his other works so far were musicianly and competent but did not yet give clear evidence of what was to come.

On the 19th October 1814, Schubert composed his setting of *Gretchen am Spinnrade* (Margaret at the Spinning Wheel) which as M. J. E. Brown puts it, is 'the appearance in music of the first German song in the sense understood today'. This poem from *Faust* was the first of Goethe's poems Schubert set, and the impact on his music of a great poet was explosive. The perennially amaz-

The main avenue of the Prater, with one of Vienna's many coffeehouses on the left, in the background

Johann Wolfgang von Goethe

ing thing about *Gretchen* is its perfection. There is nothing immature about it, nothing that suggests how early or late in his career Schubert wrote it, at seventeen or at twenty-seven. It is, for Alec Robertson, 'the answer to the question whether a perfect work of art can exist, and no one has ever challenged him on this ground. He has said the last word.'

Gretchen is grieving over her lover as she spins:

My peace is gone, my heart is heavy;
Never, never again will I find rest.
I seek only him when I look out of the window
I seek only him when I leave the house . . .

The piano part is a monotonous figure, a musical symbol of the spinning wheel; at the climax of the song, when the girl's pain is such that she stops spinning, the music stops too; then it slowly starts up again as she resumes work. The song is a beautiful distillation of a dramatically emotional moment; it is a remarkable achievement in one so young. It is no wonder that the bright young intelligentsia of Vienna was drawn to the unprepossessing-looking seventeen year-old schoolmaster who could produce such magic.

Schubert followed this Goethe song with four more by Goethe before the end of 1814; he also began his second symphony, in B flat, which he finished in March 1815.

The year 1815, during the whole of which Schubert had to teach dozens of little boys all day in his crowded home, was an extraordinary one. Always prolific, Schubert outdid himself that year,

The Jüngling was another popular coffeehouse in the city of Vienna

A fashionable promenade
on the Prater at the time
of the Congress of Vienna

and produced such a vast number of compositions it is almost
beyond comprehension. O. E. Deutsch's Thematic Catalogue lists
over 200 works for 1815 alone, and the following year was almost
as remarkable, with over 160. How a hard-pressed student-teacher
of eighteen managed to compose music of such quantity and quality
is one of the miracles of music.

In July, the most productive month of his whole life, Schubert
wrote the following songs:

2 July	*Lieb Minna* (Dear Minna)	Stadler
3 July	Salve Regina in F Major	
	Wanderers Nachtlied (Night Song of a Wanderer)	
		Goethe
	Der Fischer (The Fisherman)	Goethe
	Erster Verlust (First Loss)	Goethe
7 July	*Idens Nachtgesang* (Ida's Song of the Night)	Kosegarten
	Von Ida (from Ida)	Kosegarten
	Die Erscheinung (The Apparition)	Kosegarten
	Die Täuschung (Deception)	Kosegarten

34

	Das Sehnen (The Heart Strings)	Kosegarten
11 July	*Hymne an den Unendlichen* (Hymn to the Eternal Spirit) for Soprano, Alto, Tenor and Bass	
15 July	*Der Abend* (The Evening)	Kosegarten
	Geist der Liebe (Spirit of Love)	Kosegarten
	Tischlied (Drinking Song)	Goethe
24 July	*Abends unter der Linde* (Evening under the Lime Tree) 1st setting	Kosegarten
25 July	*Abends unter der Linde* 2nd setting	
	Das Abendrot (Evening Glow) Vocal Trio with Pianoforte	Kosegarten
	Die Mondnacht (The Moonlit Night)	Kosegarten
26 July	Started *Claudine von Villa Bella*, a three-act opera, with a libretto by Goethe	
27 July	*Huldigung* (Homage)	Kosegarten
	Alles um Liebe (All for Love)	Kosegarten

He also composed, between 24 May and 19 July, his third symphony, in D major.

That year saw in all the creation of 150 songs, a few undistinguished, many beautiful, some breath-taking. Schubert's well-known setting of Goethe's *Heidenröslein* (The Hedge Rose) is a delight; another Goethe song composed early in 1815, *Nähe des Geliebten* (The Beloved's Nearness) is a sublimely beautiful evocation of its subject matter:

I think of you when the sun's lustre
Shines from the sea;
I think of you when the moon's gleam
Reflects in wells . . .

Erlkönig, for a long time the best known, with *Gretchen*, of all Schubert's songs, was also composed in 1815, in the month of October.

What lay behind this fury of creativity one can only guess. Vienna, with its great Congress in progress, was a background that was for once politically hopeful; Schubert's new friends were enthusiastic and encouraging, and their admiration clearly inspired him. He also must have felt a great need to escape from the drab schoolroom into his magic inner world of music and, in order to achieve what he did, must have done so at every available opportunity.

There is another possible cause of this burst of creation; Schubert's emotions were in a particular state of excitement because he was in love for the first time in his life — and if his friends are to be believed, the last, for they held that Therese Grob

Ludwig Gothard Theobul Kosegarten

35

was the only serious love of his life. Anton Holzapfel met Therese Grob, the daughter of a prosperous widow with her own silk-weaving business. The Schuberts were all well-known in her house, says Holzapfel:

and in this way, on the occasion of a musical celebration for Therese's name-day in about 1811 or 1812, I too spent an evening with this family. Therese was by no means a beauty but she was well-built, rather plump and with a fresh, childlike round little face; she had a lovely soprano voice and was an accomplished singer in the Liechtental choir where, with the Schuberts and other young musical friends, I often heard her sing. Schubert wrote several things for her and in particular an enchantingly lovely Ave in C. The director of the Liechtental choir in those days was Herr Holzer, a somewhat bibulous though sound contrapuntist from whom all the Schubert brothers took music lessons. Therese's brother Heinrich who, after his mother's death, carried on the business and made a considerable position for himself as a business man, was an accomplished pianist and organist and so the Grob household opened its doors and became of importance to our Franz . . .

Holzapfel also described a lost letter dating from 1815 which Schubert had written him, in which he confessed his passion for Therese in lengthy and enthusiastic terms. Holzapfel says he wrote back dissuading him from pursuing matters 'by means of a didactic epistle which at the time seemed to me full of wisdom'. For whatever reasons, Schubert's love for Therese got no further, and in 1820 she married a master baker. One of Schubert's later friends, Anselm Hüttenbrenner, recollected in 1858 what Schubert had told him about Therese; this passage is a good example of one of the many memoirs of Schubert which had a distinct air of being senti-

A porcelain cup with Schubert's portrait; the matching saucer depicts the 'Erl King' (*Vienna, 1832*)

Therese Grob, a girl from Schubert's neighbourhood in Vienna, sang the soprano solo part in the F major Mass in 1814, the year of its composition. It is said that the young Schubert fell deeply in love with her, and that Holzapfel did his best to talk him out of his 'ridiculous infatuation'. At all events, Therese married a local master baker in 1820, and this striking portrait of her was painted in later life.

mentalized. There are inaccuracies throughout Hüttenbrenner's memoirs, but for many years what he and others like him said was taken as fact and strongly influenced nineteenth century biographies of Schubert, giving a false picture of the composer.

During a walk which I took with Schubert into the country, I asked him if he had never been in love. As he was so cold and unforthcoming towards the fair sex at parties, I was almost inclined to think he had a complete aversion for them. 'Oh no!' he said, 'I loved someone very dearly and she loved me too. She was a schoolmaster's daughter, somewhat younger than myself and in a Mass, which I composed, she sang the soprano solos most beautifully and with deep feeling. She was not exactly pretty and her face had pock-marks; but she had a heart, a heart of gold. For three years she

Anselm Hüttenbrenner (*centre*) and Johann Jenger with Schubert. This famous coloured drawing was made by Josef Teltscher in about the year 1826

hoped I would marry her; but I could not find a position which would have provided for us both. She then bowed to her parents' wishes and married someone else, which hurt me very much. I still love her and there has been no one else since who has appealed to me as much as, or more than, she. She was just not meant for me.'

Why, if his brothers could afford to marry on a teacher's stipend, could not Schubert? He was still, after all, a full-time teacher however much his heart was in music. If one looks at the poems he chose to set during this period, one sees what a large proportion are love poems; '*Love's Intoxication*', '*Frustrated Love*', '*Yearning of Love*', '*First Love*', '*All for love*', '*The Secret*' etc, etc. The themes of love are widely explored. Schubert revealed his deepest feelings in his music; perhaps he found it difficult to reveal them directly to the person he loved. Holzapfel held this view:

Schubert's feelings were violent and kept locked within himself and were certainly not without influence on his first works . . .

But Schubert, as he showed throughout his life, had the objective detachment of the true artist; he learned from his experiences, but at no time is it safe to assume that the profound statements on the human condition he makes in his music are in any way a literal comment on his own life.

Throughout 1815 and most of 1816 Schubert lived at home, and continued to compose prolifically. He wrote two more symphonies in 1816 — the fourth in C minor (he later named this the Tragic) in the spring, and the fifth in B flat in September and October. These symphonies appear to have been performed, soon after composition, by an amateur orchestra which had grown out of the Schubert family quartet. Schubert played the viola in this orchestra.

The early symphonies, like the early quartets, though in the familiar idiom of the day, are not in the least imitative of Haydn, Mozart or Beethoven. They are the work of a young genius whose instrumental music already contains all the special characteristics so typical of later Schubert: the beautiful melodies, for instance, which are developed in his own particular manner unlike that of anyone else. The authentic emotional *voice* of Schubert is already clear, but does not have the richness yet which comes from deepened thought and experience.

Besides the symphonies Schubert also composed over 100 songs, the cantata *Prometheus*, much church music including a Mass (No. 4 in C major) and many sonatas and dances. The songs include settings of poems by his new friends Mayrhofer and Schober, and most famous of all songs written that year, the exquisite lullaby *Wiegenlied* (Cradlesong). (His father's family had increased by two new babies, one born in April 1815 and one in December 1816.)

'Game of Ball at Atzenbrugg' — a joint effort by Schober, who drew the landscape and architecture, and Schwind who drew the figures. In the foreground can be seen Schubert, with his long pipe, Schober reclining on the grass and Kraissl playing the violin. Atzenbrugg Castle is in the background (*see page 79*)

The dances he wrote in response to the insatiable Viennese demand for them. 'He himself never danced,' wrote a friend, 'but was always ready to sit down at the piano, where for hours he improvised the most beautiful waltzes; those he liked he repeated, in order to remember them and write them down afterwards.'

Early in 1816 Schubert applied for a music master's post in Laibach, Carniola (now in Yugoslavia and known as Ljubljana); not only did it carry a far better salary than Schubert received as sixth assistant in the bottom form of his father's school, but it also had the attraction of teaching the one subject he loved. Months later he heard he had been unsuccessful. It must have been growing plain to him that his music and his job as a schoolmaster could not co-exist for much longer. It is a pity that the entries in a journal Schubert kept during 1816 are not more revealing of his life and its problems. The style of these few entries is formal and stiff, not at all like the easy ebullience of his letters.

Open-air dancing on the Prater

40

A view of Döbling by the composer's brother Karl, who was a gifted illustrator and landscape artist

15th June 1816

I took an evening walk for once, as I had not done for several months. There can be scarcely anything more agreeable than to enjoy the green country on an evening after a hot summer's day, a pleasure for which the fields between Währing and Döbling seem to have been especially created. In the uncertain twilight and in the company of my brother Karl, my heart warmed within me, 'How beautiful,' I thought and exclaimed, standing still delightedly. A graveyard close by reminded us of our dear mother. Thus, talking sadly and intimately, we arrived at the point where the Döbling road divides.

The same slightly unctuous and sentimental tone is found in his description of his teacher Salieri's celebration of the fiftieth anniversary of his arrival in Vienna:

16th June 1816

It must be beautiful and refreshing for an artist to see all his pupils gathered about him, each one striving to give of his best for his jubilee, and to hear in all these compositions the expression of pure nature, free from all the eccentricity that is common among most composers nowadays, and is due almost wholly to one of our greatest German artists; that eccentricity which joins and confuses the tragic with the comic, the agreeable with the repulsive, heroism with howlings and the holiest with harlequinades, without distinction, so as to goad people to madness instead of dissolving them in love, to incite them to laughter instead of lifting them up to God. To see this eccentricity banished from the circle of his pupils and instead to look upon pure, holy nature, must be the greatest pleasure for an artist who, guided by such a one as Gluck, learned to know nature and to uphold it in spite of the unnatural conditions of our age.

This description is clearly of Beethoven whose style did not appeal to Salieri, and here Schubert is young enough still to be swayed by

41

Ferdinand Schubert, born in 1794

his eloquent opinions on the dangers of German 'eccentricity'. It is possible, however, that there were aspects of Beethoven's genius that did disturb Schubert then, if not later.

The longest entry in his journal is on 8 September when, after an evening at Mayrhofer's lodgings, he wrote this passage of random thoughts, ideas and youthful paradoxes.

Natural disposition and education determine mankind's mind and heart. The heart *is* the ruler, but the mind *ought* to be. Take people as they are, not as they should be.

Blissful moments brighten this dark life; up there these blissful moments become continual joy, and happier ones still will turn into visions of yet happier worlds, and so on.

Happy he who finds a true man-friend. Happier still he who finds a true friend in his wife.

To a free man matrimony is a terrifying thought in these days: he exchanges it either for melancholy or for crude sensuality. Monarchs of today, you see this and are silent. Or do you not see it? If so, O God, shroud our senses and feelings in numbness; yet take back the veil again one day without lasting harm.

Man bears misfortune without complaint, but feels it the more keenly. — Wherefore did God give us compassion?

Light mind, light heart. Too light a mind usually means too heavy a heart.

Urban politeness is a mighty antithesis to the sincerity of human relationships.

The greatest misfortune of the wise and the greatest fortune of the foolish rest upon convention.

To be noble and unhappy is to feel the full depths of misfortune and happiness, just as to be noble and happy is to feel happiness and misfortune.

Karl Schubert, born in 1795

The list then breaks off suddenly and Schubert's own lighthearted voice is heard at last:

I can't think of any more now. Tomorrow I shall think of something more.

He ends with an irreverent (and irrelevant) rhyme:

What are all these questions?
'Twill not do to dare it.
No, 'tis not enough:

We must grin and bear it.
   And so to bed
   Till morn shines red.

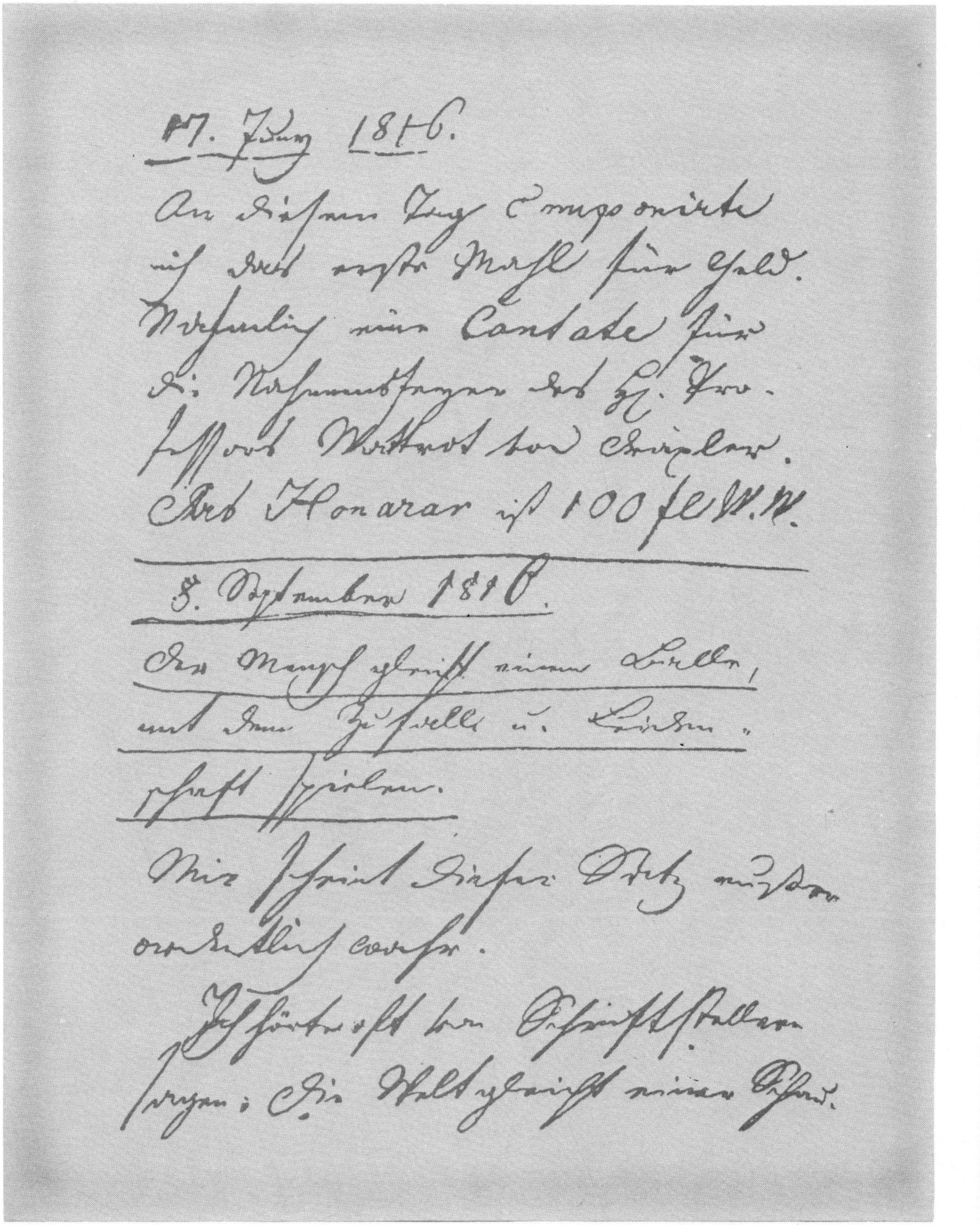

17. Juny 1816.

An diesem Tage componirte
ich das erste Mahl für Geld.
Nehmlich eine Cantate für
die Nahmensfeyer des Hr. Hr.
Josseph Watteroth von Dráxler.
Das Honorar ist 100 fl W.W.

_____

8. September 1816.

Der Mensch gleicht einer Ball,
mit dem Zufall u. Leiden-
schaft spielen.

_____

Mir scheint dieser Satz außer-
ordentlich wahr.

Ich hörte oft von Schriftstellern
sagen: Die Welt gleicht einer Schau-

Sketch of Schubert, by Moritz von Schwind

Chapter 4

The Taste of Freedom

'There has never been a more spontaneous artist; never one, whose pages, in the old phrase, smelled less of the lamp.'—Desmond Shawe-Taylor

In the autumn of 1816 Schubert broke free of schoolmastering; he moved into Schober's family apartment in the Landskrongasse, and remained there for the next year. Schober's mother and his sister Sophie were friendly and welcoming; the arrangement appears to have worked well. Schubert cannot but have felt a profound sense of liberation; none of the hated drudgery of teaching small boys, none of the continual pressures of the overcrowded family home, no more living cheek by jowl with his father, whose pro-Emperor, pro-Metternich patriotism and whose disapproval of music as a way of life must have irked Schubert. To escape into the freedom of the Schober establishment with his days to spend as he pleased was heaven indeed.

Schubert loved Schober with all his heart. His cosmopolitan background, his width of interests, his liveliness, his wit, all made up for what other people saw as amoral shallowness. Of all Schubert's friends, posterity has given Franz Schober the worst press: partly because men in their circle who later on in life became famous grew to dislike him, and partly because Schober himself never put the balance right by writing down his memories of life with Schubert. In 1869 he stated rather pathetically in response to a letter from Schubert's future friend, Bauernfeld:

With the best will in the world I cannot fulfil your request, so natural and just, to write out some Schubertiana for you. I have already tried to do it so often for myself; I should so much have liked to write a little book about him and our life together, and I have never accomplished it. How could I make clear to you the insuperable inability to write? Make clear to you, who write so easily and so excellently, the inability which has pursued me to the point of desperation throughout my life and which, as a matter of fact, is the cause of unhappiness in me. But there it is! I will gladly tell you all I know, when we meet, but write it down I cannot . . . Do not think it is lack of goodwill or indolence that prevents me, but there it is.

43

Although Schubert's life was so excellently documented by word and picture by his friends, the lack of anything from Schober is a real loss. He clearly shared many of Schubert's secrets, and knew about his love-life (he refers in 1869 to 'a love story of Schubert's which not a soul knows, as I am the only one in the secret and J

The manuscript of 'An Die Musik'

Schubert, as depicted in portrait by Leroux

The Mayrhofer song "Am Erlaf-see," Schubert's first published work

have told it to nobody'), but not a whisper of any facts has come down to us. That the two of them indulged later on in a night-life which led to Schubert's catching syphilis, and that many people described Schober as amoral and irreligious is fact. He was a complete antidote to Schubert's prim and religious father, and in this alone was important in rounding out Schubert's ideas and experience of life.

Music continued to pour out in these new surroundings. In March 1817 he composed *An Die Musik* (To Music) to a poem of Schober's. It was a particularly creative period; the month before he had composed amongst other things *Der Tod und das Mädchen* (Death and the Maiden) and soon after it *Die Forelle* (The Trout), both masterpieces whose themes he used again successfully later in a quartet and a quintet.

An Die Musik is a rapt hymn to the power of music, and is a perfect achievement. *Du holde Kunst*, wrote Schober,

Oh dearest art, how often, in hours of sadness,
When life has caught me in its cruel trap
Have you inspired new love in my heart
And carried me into a far better world!

Often a soft note, rising from your harp
A sweet and holy chord sent from you
Has given me heavenly visions of happier times.
O dearest art — for this I thank you now.

This simple, rather sentimental, poem, with its image so beloved of the Romantic age, of the Aeolian harp, was made by Schobert into a heartrending, beautiful song. If only for this work of art, Schubert and Schober's friendship would be remembered. Alec Robertson has not put it too highly by saying:

It is the song above all others which floats into the memory when one stands before Schubert's grave; it is the song a musician would wish to be sung at his own passing; every bar and phrase of it is immortal.

Since in Schubert's hands the German *Lied* came of age, it is important to understand a little of its history in order to see this achievement in perspective. The solo song has a long history; ballads and folk song sung by minstrels and bards are part of Western culture's early development. The *Lied* grew out of folk song; even as early as the thirteenth century, the poet and composer Walther von der Vogelweide was writing songs with a powerful melodic line, songs which influenced his successors and became part of the German heritage. Schubert's immediate predecessors, J. F. Reichardt and J. Zumsteeg, both made their own innovations:

the former showed that accompaniments to a strophic song need not be meagre but descriptive and picturesque, and that the *strophes* (verses) themselves could be widely varied; the latter made the accompaniment of ballads dramatic, with effective declamation and sensitively composed harmony.

But two strong reasons for the rise of the *Lied* coincided with Schubert's life — the new German Romantic poetry led by the giant figure of Goethe, and the eclipse of the harpsichord by the fortepiano. We have seen the effect on Schubert of his first reading of Goethe's *Faust*. A miraculous new development in song occurred when *Gretchen am Spinnrade* was composed. To quote Robertson again, Schubert endowed

the piano accompaniment with the wealth of expression instrumental music had so far achieved. He opens — and this is the important point — a new page of musical psychology . . . At a time when his symphonies and chamber music are immature, his solo piano-writing equally so, he produces a piano part, beautifully fitted to the instrument, which is of symphonic importance . . .

Schubert, influenced by the orchestral treatment of arias in Gluck and above all by Mozart's operas, transferred this richness to the piano part. This lyric/dramatic fusion was absolutely new. It is in the *setting* of his melodies that Schubert's supreme achievement lies; the fusing of voice with piano into a perfect lyrical and dramatic whole.

A detail from a somewhat romanticised painting in the Mansell collection showing Schubert at work

'Death and the Maiden': steel engraving by Max Klinger

Schubert loved the piano, and in his day the Viennese fortepiano was a sophisticated and sensitive instrument at its peak of development. Vienna was experiencing a golden age of music; the list of composers who lived in Vienna or made their reputation there between 1770 and 1830 is long; as well as the four great masters,

there were Weber, Czerny, Hummel, Schumann, Chopin and many more. During those sixty years in that city works were composed which for most people are the 'greatest' in music — *Fidelio*, *Die Zauberflöte*, Beethoven's and Schubert's Ninth Symphonies, the Missa Solemnis, Schubert's C major Quintet, Mozart's Requiem — as the list continues one can only marvel at its richness.

It is not surprising that such a musical city should be well served by its instrument makers. The piano played the most important role in Viennese musical circles, whether they were bourgeois, bohemian, aristocratic or professional. Standards achieved by the famous Viennese piano makers of the time, like Stein, Graf and Streicher, were second to none. Mozart wrote an enthusiastic letter to his father describing why he loved a Stein piano:

I can do what I like with the keys — the tone is always equal. It does not tinkle disagreeably. It has neither the fault of being too loud nor too soft . . . in a word the tone is perfectly equal throughout . . . his pianos are really solid.

Mozart goes on to describe Stein's perfection of craftsmanship, how he exposed the piano soundboard to all weathers in order to make it crack if it was going to; 'then he glues in slivers of wood so that it becomes completely solid and resistant . . .'

The Viennese piano reached its apogee in those years; it could not be developed further because its action, which worked on a much simpler principle than English or French pianos, had reached its limits of perfection and could not be adapted further to accommodate the needs of later nineteenth century romantic composers.

The pianos of the early 1800s were expressive, but the new composers (except Schubert) wanted power as well. Beethoven and Liszt literally demolished pianos when they played their own works on them. A visitor to Beethoven described the state of his piano:

What a spectacle offered itself to my view — there was no sound in the treble, and broken strings were mixed up like a thorn bush after a gale.

The modern grand piano developed from the stronger and more adaptable French and English pianos, while the Viennese piano, with its limitations, disappeared from the musical scene. It is only recently that interest in it has reawakened, and faithful copies are being made from Steins and Grafs still in existence. The sound is

Schubert's fortepiano
(*Schubert Museum*)

A Graf fortepiano of
1826

very different from that of a modern piano; Kenneth van Barthold
describes it as:

. . . silvery, fragile, and yet with great carrying power and clarity of line.
Moreover, the relationship between its various registers, the bottom, the
middle and the top, is quite different from that of today's instruments. To
play Mozart, Haydn or early Beethoven on one is to feel difficulties of
balance and legato disappear under one's fingers: the melodies sing out
over the accompaniment . . . for the music written with its sound in mind
it has no peer, and our modern piano is a very poor substitute.

Schubert had very strong ideas about pianos and the playing of
them. He loved the sound as it was, and did not hanker after more
power. In a letter written to his parents from Steyr, where he was
on holiday in 1825, he wrote of his dislike of the romantic style of
piano-playing:

I cannot endure the accursed chopping in which even distinguished
pianoforte players indulge and which delights neither the ear nor the
mind.

In the same letter he says 'several people assured me that the keys

View of Steyr, engraving by Johann Poppel from a sketch by Ludwig Rohbock

Part of manuscript for "Antigone und Oedip,"
with ornamentations used by the singer Vogl

became singing voices under my hands', while in another letter written that same summer to his brother Ferdinand he says of his *Lieder* recitals: 'The manner in which Vogl sings and the way I accompany, as though we were one at such a moment, is something quite new and unheard-of for these people.'

If we see those remarks against the sound of a true Viennese piano, we come nearer to Schubert's own conception of his *Lieder*. That the accompaniment should be 'at one' with the voice part, but *not* subservient to it, is crucial; music and poetry are fused into a new whole.

Two of Schubert's friends have left us descriptions of his attitude to the piano and the way in which voice and piano should be united. Albert Stadler, an old friend of seminary days wrote:

To see and hear him play his own pianoforte compositions was a real pleasure. A beautiful touch, a quiet hand, clear, neat playing, full of insight and feeling. He still belonged to the old school of good pianoforte players, whose fingers had not yet begun to attack the poor keys like birds of prey.

Leopold Sonnleithner described in fascinating detail, in his memoirs of 1857, the way Schubert liked his songs to be sung:

As regards the way in which Schubert's songs should be performed, there are very strange opinions today amongst the great majority of people. Most of them think they have achieved the summit if they interpret the songs in the manner they imagine to be the *dramatic*. According to this, there is as much declamation as possible, sometimes whispered, sometimes with passionate outbursts, with retarding of the tempo, etc. — I can only say that I am always apprehensive when it is announced at a party that Schubert's songs are going to be sung, for even quite capable and, in their way, musically cultured ladies and gentlemen usually sin cruelly against poor Schubert. I heard him accompany and rehearse his songs more than a hundred times. Above all, he always kept the most strict and even time, except in the few cases where he had expressly indicated in writing a ritardando, morendo, accelerando etc. Furthermore he never allowed violent expression in performance. The Lieder-singer, as a rule, only relates experiences and feelings of others; he does not himself impersonate the characters whose feelings he describes. Poet, composer and singer must conceive the song *lyrically*, not *dramatically*. With Schubert especially, the true expression, the deepest feeling is already inherent in the melody as such, as is admirably enhanced by the accompaniment. Everything that hinders the flow of the melody and disturbs the evenly flowing accompaniment is, therefore, exactly contrary to the composer's intention and destroys the musical effect.

By 1817, Schubert had produced so many masterpieces in song that his friends began an effort to spread his fame beyond their own small circle. Spaun had already, in 1816, tried to boost Schubert's name by sending an album of the Goethe settings to the great poet himself, accompanied by a letter begging Goethe's permission to dedicate to him a planned edition of these songs. Goethe did not answer the letter, but he did at least return the songs. Undeterred, Spaun and Schober pressed on with their friend's cause.

There was in Vienna a famous singer called Johann Michael Vogl (1768-1840) whose high baritone voice was a star attraction at the Vienna Court Opera. Spaun tells us the story:

Schubert, who always had to sing his own songs, now frequently expressed a great desire to find a singer for his songs, and his old wish to get to know the Court opera singer, Vogl, grew stronger and stronger. It was now decided in our little circle that Vogl must be won over for the Schubert

Leopold von
Sonnleithner: oil painting
usually attributed to
Kupelwieser, 1828

52

The Vienna Opera
House

songs. The task was a hard one, as Vogl was very difficult to approach.

Schober's sister, who died young, had been married to the singer Siboni, and Schober still had some connections with the theatre, which made an approach to Vogl easier for him. He told Vogl, with glowing enthusiasm, about Schubert's beautiful compositions and invited him to try them out. Vogl replied that he was fed to the teeth with music, that he had been brought up on music and was far more concerned to get free of it than to get to know any new music. He had heard about young geniuses hundreds of times and had always been disappointed, and this was certain to be the case with Schubert too. He wanted to be left in peace and wished to hear nothing more about it. — This refusal upset us all deeply, all except Schubert, who said he had expected just such an answer and found it perfectly understandable.

Meanwhile Vogl was approached repeatedly by Schober, and by others as well, and finally he promised to come to Schober's one evening to see what it was all about, as he put it.

He made his appearance at Schober's at the appointed hour, quite majestically, and when the small, insignificant Schubert made a somewhat awkward bow and, in his embarrassment, stammered some incoherent words about the honour of the acquaintance, Vogl turned up his nose rather contemptuously and the beginning of the acquaintance seemed to us to portend disaster. Finally Vogl said, 'Let's see what you have got there; accompany me,' and thereupon he took up the nearest sheet of music, containing Mayrhofer's poem 'Augenlied', a pretty, very melodious, but not important song. Vogl hummed rather than sang, and then said coldly, 'Not bad'. When, after that, 'Memnon', 'Ganymed', and other songs were accompanied for him, all of which, however, he only sang mezza-voce, he

53

became more and more friendly, though he went away without promising to come again. On leaving he clapped Schubert on the shoulders and said to him, 'There is something in you but you are too little of a comedian, too little of a showman; you squander your fine thoughts without making the best of them'. To others Vogl expressed himself considerably more favourably about Schubert than he did to the latter and his closest friends. (When the song *'Die Dioskuren'* came to his notice he declared it to be a magnificent song and said it was frankly incomprehensible how such depth and maturity could emanate from the little young man.) The impression the songs made on him was an overwhelming one and he now approached our circle again of his own accord, invited Schubert to his home, rehearsed songs with him and when he realised the tremendous, overwhelming impression his performance made on us, on Schubert himself and on every kind of audience, he grew so enthusiastic about the songs that he himself now became Schubert's most ardent admirer, and instead of giving up this music, as he had previously intended, his enthusiasm for it was kindled anew.

This meeting, and the genuine friendship that grew up between Schubert and Vogl, seemingly such disparate characters, was of incalculable importance to Schubert. Vogl was an influential person in the music world; by singing this unknown composer's songs he made them famous, in time, all over Austria. He was a most interesting man, tall, commanding, well-educated and uncommonly well-read. He read Greek and Latin with ease and was also fluent in English. Schubert spent a great deal of time in his company and was profoundly influenced by Vogl's steady personality, and genuine culture. Being championed by a man as established and admired as Vogl was an encouragement in itself.

They were a comic pair: Vogl was immensely tall, and Schubert was under five foot. (His smallness also had its lucky side, because it made him ineligible for national service.) There is a witty sketch by Schober of enormous Vogl stalking proudly, and tiny Schubert behind him, a roll of music under his arm and another bulging out of his pocket; Schubert has a slightly surprised expression.

Important as Vogl was to Schubert in every way, he did him one bad turn. He never really understood Schubert's working methods, so during Schubert's lifetime, and even more damagingly after his death, he spread about the idea that Schubert was a 'clairvoyant' composer. His wife Kunigonde (whom he married in 1826 and who never got on well with Schubert) wrote condescendingly in 1850:

And Vogl was always of the opinion that Schubert was in a trance-like state whenever he composed. In this way one can also explain how, in this state of clairvoyance the scarcely educated boy, and later the only moderately educated youth, had glimpses into the secrets of life, feeling and knowledge.

Franz von Schober

Schober's famous cartoon
of Vogl and Schubert

Albert Stadler gave a similar version of Vogl's viewpoint:

Vogl once wrote to me, on some special occasion or other, 'There are two kinds of composition, one which, as in Schubert's case, comes into existence during a state of clairvoyance or somnambulism, without any conscious action on the part of the composer, but inevitably, by act of providence and inspiration. The second way of composing is through will-power, reflection, effort, knowledge, etc.'

This 'second way' is as much part of Schubert as of any great composer; but his speed and prodigious output puzzled his friends. That conception that Schubert was a clairvoyant, a 'natural', a vehicle almost, took a long time to die, particularly as his extant

55

manuscripts were mainly fair copies — and 'fair' in every sense — so they looked as if the music had indeed been 'dictated' to Schubert. But sketches and first manuscripts have been discovered to prove for ever that although Schubert was an amazingly spontaneous and prolific composer, there was nothing facile or accidental in his creative effort.

Spaun's spirited defence of his friend, written in 1886 to correct these serious misapprehensions, disposes once and for all of the illusion that Schubert was a clairvoyant with no real education:

His unprecedented, inexhaustible wealth of melody was a divine gift, and this cannot be acquired even through the greatest skill and learning in thorough-bass. But anyone inclined to believe that Schubert was only an excellent natural composer . . . would make a great mistake. He possessed the most thorough musical knowledge and had studied the works of the great masters, both old and new, in the greatest detail. Bach and Handel he worked through thoroughly and held in very high esteem; all Gluck's operas he could play almost from memory and there was probably not a note by Mozart, Beethoven and Haydn that he did not know. With such knowledge one is no mere natural composer.

Chapter 5

A Journey to Hungary

'The State should keep me,' Schubert sometimes said to me, 'I have come into the world for no purpose but to compose!' — Josef Hüttenbrenner

In August 1817 Schubert had to leave the Schober household because his room was needed for a member of the family. He returned for the time being to the restrictions of the school house, but does not appear to have taken up teaching again. He had composed much during his stay at Schober's: nearly 60 songs, two overtures in the Italian style (Rossini was the rage in Vienna), seven piano sonatas, and several groups of dances. He began working on his sixth symphony in C major after he returned home, finishing it in February 1818. This is one of the least interesting of his symphonies, though it shows great technical advances; as M. J. E. Brown says: 'The use of the orchestra is masterly, the movements are expertly organized to the point of glibness, all is crisp and competent. But there is no heart in the work; it is all externals. The expert craftsmanship is used on unattractive, trivial material . . .' Soon after he finished this symphony, Schubert began another, in D, and voluminous sketches for this exist. They show very clearly how Schubert worked, developing rhythms, scraps of tune, harmonic figures; but he rejected this mass of work for reasons we do not know, and did not return to it.

Schubert's circle of friends was growing, and one gets a sense of cheerful ebullience and humour from the many affectionate and lighthearted dedications he wrote on manuscripts given to his friends. 'Written down for my coffee, wine and punch brother, Anselm Hüttenbrenner'; another is inflated Latin, which ends: 'Servorum servo Francisco Seraphico vulgo Schubert nominato'. The Hüttenbrenners became close to Schubert at this time: Anselm (1794-1868), a fellow composer, and his younger brother Josef (1796-1882). Schubert wrote a short note to Josef after consuming large amounts of red Hungarian wine in Anselm's company.

Dearest friend
  It gives me extraordinary pleasure to know you like my songs. As a proof

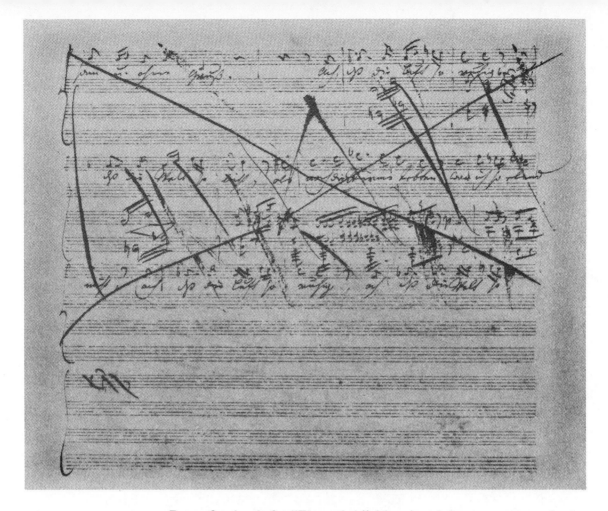

Page of a sketch for "Einsamkeit" (above) and the same passage, beginning with the second measure of the sketch, in the first printed edition (below)

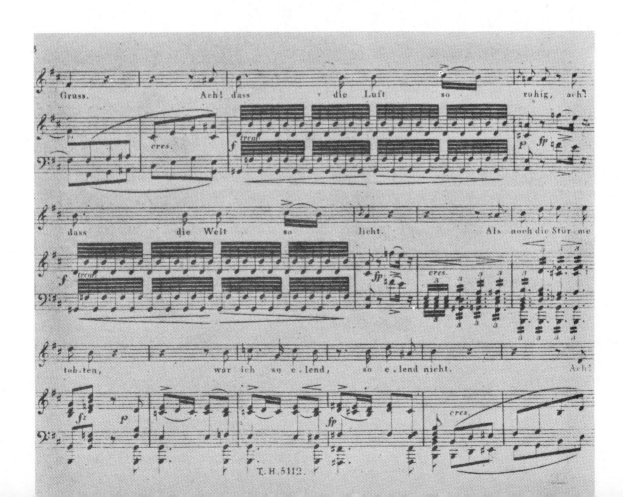

A dedication copy of "Die Forelle" (above) and the first publication of that song (below)

Anselm Hüttenbrenner

of my most devoted friendship I am sending you another, which I have just now written out at Anselm Hüttenbrenner's at midnight . . .

Just as, in my haste, I was going to send the thing, I rather sleepily took up the inkwell and poured it quite calmly over it. What a disaster!

Schubert had intended to pick up the sandbox. The ink-blotted manuscript of *Die Forelle* was in the Hüttenbrenners' possession for many years, and was reproduced and then unaccountably lost. (The Hüttenbrenners' most appalling carelessness, however, was over the manuscript of Schubert's opera *Claudine von Villa Bella*, a large part of which was used by Anselm's servants to light fires.)

During the course of 1818 Schubert's output decreased considerably; he wrote only sixteen songs that year, none of them amongst his masterpieces, varied piano music — duets, fantasias, sonatas —

and the usual crop of dances. One of the reasons for this decrease was travel. In July he left the Vienna area for the first time and went to Hungary for five months, to become music tutor to the two young daughters of Count Johann Karl Esterházy at their summer castle of Zseliz. Schubert wrote enthusiastically to Vienna:

Zseliz, 3rd August 1818.

Best and dearest friends,

How could I forget you, you who mean everything to me? How are you, Spaun, Schober, Mayrhofer, Senn? Are you well? I am quite well. I live and compose like a god, as though that were as it should be.

Mayrhofer's 'Solitude' ('*Einsamkeit*') is ready, and I believe it to be the best I have done, for I was without a care. I hope that you are all merry and in the best of health, as I am. Thank God I live at last, and it was high time, otherwise I should have become nothing but a thwarted musician. Schober had better pay my respects to Herr Vogl, to whom I will soon take the liberty of writing. If possible, make him consider if he will not be so kind as to sing one of my songs at the Kunz concert in November — whichever he likes. Greetings to all the acquaintances you can think of . . . Write to me soon, for I cherish every syllable from you all.

Since Schubert travelled very little during his short life, and never further than Zseliz, letters to his friends and family at home in Vienna are rare and welcome. Towards the end of August he wrote a long and revealing letter to Ferdinand:

Kick my city friends mightily, or have them kicked, to make them write to me. Tell Mother that my laundry is very well looked after, and that her motherly care greatly touches me. (But if I could have more apparel, I should be extremely glad if you were to send me an extra supply of

The Bailiff's lodge at Zseliz, where Schubert stayed during his first visit to the Esterhazy estate

The main chateau of the Esterházys at Zseliz

handkerchieves, scarves and stockings. Also I am much in need of two pairs of — cashmere trousers, for which Hart may take the measure where he will. I should send the money for them at once.) My receipts for the month of July, including the travelling expenses, amounted to 200 florins. — It is beginning to get cold here already, yet we shall not leave for Vienna before the middle of November. I hope next month to go for a few weeks to Freistadtl, which belongs to Count Erdödy, my count's uncle. They say the country there is extraordinarily pretty. I also hope to get to Pest, as we are going for the vintage to Pócs-Megyer, which is not far from it . . . But altogether I look forward to all the vintages, about which I have been told a lot of such nice things. The harvest too is very fine here. The corn is not put into barns here, as in Austria, but enormous stacks are erected, which they call *Tristen*. They are often some 80 to 100 yards long and 100 to 120 feet high. They are stacked with such skill that the rain, which is made to run off, can do no damage. Oats and the like are buried in the earth, too. — Well and happy as I am here, and kind as the people are, I look forward with immense pleasure to the moment at which the word will be 'To Vienna, to Vienna!' Indeed, beloved Vienna, thou holdest all that is most dear and cherished in thy narrow space, and nothing but the sight of thee, the heavenly sight, will appease my yearning . . .

Another lively and even more revealing letter was written to his band of friends:

8 Sept. 1818

Dear Schober, dear Spaun, dear Mayrhofer et al.

How infinitely the letters from you, all and sundry, delight me is inexpressible! I was just attending a deal in oxen and cows when your nice, portly letter was handed to me. As I broke it open, loud cries of joy burst from me on beholding the name of Schober. I read it in a neighbouring room, with continual laughter and childish pleasure. It was as though I were laying my hands on my dear friends themselves. But I will answer you in good order:

Dear Schobert,
    I see we shall have to keep this transformation of the name. Well then, dear Schobert, your letter was very welcome and precious to me from beginning to end . . .

After a long passage for Schober, he adds:

Now a description for everybody: Our castle is not one of the largest, but very neatly built. It is surrounded by a most beautiful garden. I live at the steward's quarters. It is fairly quiet, save for some forty geese, which at times cackle so lustily together that one cannot hear oneself speak. Good people around me, all of them. It must be rare for a Count's retinue to fit so well together as these do. The inspector, a Slavonian, is a good fellow, and has a great opinion of his former musical talents. He still blows two German dances in 3-4 time on the flute, with great virtuosity. His son studies philosophy, is here on holiday just now, and I hope I shall take to him. His wife is a woman like all women who want to be ladies. The steward fits his office perfectly: a man with an extraordinary insight into his pockets and bags. The doctor, who is really accomplished, ails like an old lady at the age of 24. Very unnatural. The surgeon, whom I like best, is a venerable old man of 75, always cheerful and happy. May God give every one so happy an old age! The magistrate is an unassuming, excellent man. A companion of the Count, a merry old fellow and a capable musician, often keeps me company. The cook, the lady's maid, the chambermaid, the nurse, the manager, &c, and two grooms are all good folk. The cook rather a rake; the lady's maid 30 years of age; the chambermaid very pretty and often my companion; the nurse a good old thing; the manager my rival. The two grooms are more fit for traffic with horses than with human beings. The Count is rather rough, the Countess haughty but more sensitive; the little countesses are nice children. So far I have been spared dining with the family. Now I cannot think of any more; I hardly need tell you, who know me, that with my natural candour I hit it off quite well with all these people.

    It is not clear how close a relationship he had with the chambermaid he mentions. That Schubert had an earthy and sensual side to his nature is stated by many of his friends, and he gives hints of it in his letters. There is a letter to his brothers in which he tells Ignaz (who hated priests) about the local clergy:

But you have no conception what a gang the priesthood is here: bigoted as mucky old cattle, stupid as arch donkeys and boorish as bisons . . . They chuck about blackguards, riffraff, etc from the pulpit, something lovely; they put a death's head on the pulpit and say, 'Look here, you pockmarked mugs, that's how you will look one day.' Or else: 'There, a fellow takes a slut into a tavern, they dance all night, then they go to bed tight, and when they get up there are three of 'em.' etc.

There was no one in Zseliz Schubert could confide in:

Not a soul here has any feeling for true art, or at most the Countess now and again (unless I am wrong). So I am alone with my beloved and have to hide her in my room, in my pianoforte and in my bosom. Although this often makes me sad, on the other hand it elevates me the more. Have no fear, then, that I shall stay away longer than is absolutely necessary. Several songs have materialized these days — very good ones, I hope.

Countess Karoline
Esterházy

He returned thankfully to Vienna towards the end of November. Michael Vogl showed his pleasure at his young protégé's return by introducing him to the directors of the Kärntnertor Theatre (the Court Theatre) who asked him to compose a one act opera. Schubert obliged with *Die Zwillingsbrüder* (The Twin Brothers), a comic *Singspiel* (Song and dialogue) about the alternating reappearance of twin brothers upsetting the affairs of their old village until, in a grand C major finale, all the problems are sorted out and the brothers are united. Vogl played both brothers. It is a light work with some attractive music amongst the ten sung numbers, but its performance was delayed for over a year because Rossini, then the most celebrated of Italian opera composers, arrived in Vienna and all the opera houses played nothing but Rossini in a fury of adulation.

Vienna was always opera-mad, and Schubert knew that the only way for a composer to achieve fame and fortune was to compose a popular opera. Throughout his life he devoted much time, energy and enthusiasm to composing operas; he wrote seventeen in all, of which only three ever reached the stage. For instance, in that extra-

Vienna, the Imperial Court Theatre by the Kärtnerthor where *Die Zwillingsbrüder* was first produced (*coloured engraving: anonymous*)

Playbill for *Die Zwillingsbrüder*

ordinarily productive year 1815 he had worked on no fewer than *seven* operas, none of them commissioned and none performed. The best was the ill-fated *Claudine von Villa Bella*, with a libretto by Goethe.

Schubert was determined to succeed at opera as this fury of activity shows, and with an actual commission from the Kärntnertor Theatre he felt he had arrived at last. A performance, sung by Vogl, was assured. Another commission, to compose *Die Zauberharfe* (The Magic Harp) for the rival Theater an der Wien was in the offing. But in the event, the performance of *Die Zwillingsbrüder* did not take place until the spring of 1820, was not very successful, and was withdrawn after only six performances. A review in the *Allgemeine Musikalische Zeitung* in June 1820 said:

The music for The Twin Brothers has much originality and many interesting passages and the declamation is correct; but it is a blot on the work that the sentiments of simple country folk are interpreted much too seriously, not to say heavy-handedly, for a comic subject.

Opera had strict conventions, and they hampered Schubert all his life.

When Schubert returned to Vienna in November 1818 it was not to his father's house, but to lodgings with the poet Mayrhofer. Josef von Spaun says they lived 'for a few years in the same room, under the care of the excellent widow Sanssouci, who tried to keep things reasonably tidy for the two somewhat unpractical gentlemen.' Mayrhofer's description of their ménage, written soon after his friend's death, highlights its inevitable drawbacks as well as its advantages.

While we lived together our idiosyncracies could not but show themselves; we were both richly endowed in that respect, and the consequences could not fail to appear. We teased each other in many different ways and turned our sharp edges on each other to our mutual amusement and pleasure. His happy and comfortable sensuousness and my introspective nature were thus thrown into higher relief . . .

Falsity and envy were utter strangers to him; his character was a mixture of tenderness and coarseness, sensuality and candour, sociability and melancholy.

Mayrhofer's introspective gloom, his bad health and hypochondria made him a difficult man to live with. He was a civil servant, employed oddly enough as a censor of books; he was 'gruff, sickly and irritable — deep and full of ideas — never laughing or joking, disdainful of women and frivolity — whist, his sole amusement.' He was a strange companion for the sociable, hedonistic Schubert, but perhaps it was an attraction of opposites.

At all events, they shared a room until 1820; Schubert had a piano at his disposal and was able to work in the manner which suited him best. Schubert liked to work on getting up in the morning right through until the early afternoon, when he would go out to meet friends in a coffeehouse, then walk, pay visits, make music, go to the opera, and then finish the evening having supper in one of Vienna's many inns where more friends would join them. This pattern of existence was obviously ideal for him, and he did not like to break it by giving such tedious and time-consuming

Löus coffeehouse in Vienna: a contemporary print

A typical Viennese inn scene (*from a painting by Neder*)

things as music lessons. His friend Leopold Sonnleithner, a member of a highly musical and cultured Viennese family, wrote despairingly of his habits:

Schubert was extraordinarily fertile and industrious in composing. For everything else that goes by the name of *work* he had no use. Seldom going to the theatre or into fashionable society, he loved to spend the evening at an inn, in the company of lively friends, and on such occasions midnight often passed unnoticed and pleasure was indulged to excess. As a result of this he acquired the habit of staying in bed in the morning until 10 or 11 o'clock; and as this was the time when he felt the greatest urge to compose, the morning hours passed in this way, and the best time for earning some money by teaching was thus lost.'

Poor Sonnleithner found Schubert's bohemian side difficult to accept; these memoirs, too, were written at the height of the nineteenth century when the moral climate was distinctly cooler.

68

Having bewailed Schubert's lack of business sense and punctuality, Sonnleithner goes on to discuss Schubert's drinking habits, and says that although Schubert was very fond of wine he did not usually overdo it:

But unfortunately I must confess that I saw him in a drunken state several times. On one occasion I was with him at a party, in one of the suburbs, where there was a great deal of music-making and feasting. I went home at about 2 o'clock in the morning; Schubert remained still longer and the next day I learnt that he had to sleep there as he was incapable of going home. This happened in a house where he had not long been known and where he had only been introduced a short time previously.

But Schubert cannot have drunk to excess very frequently; if he had, he would have lacked the clarity of mind needed to compose the enormous amount he did in his short life.

Vogl's affection for and interest in Schubert is shown again in the summer of 1819, when he took Schubert away with him to spend the holidays in his home town of Steyr. It was the first of several successful holidays they spent together, usually at Vogl's expense. The disparity between their ages and backgrounds did not matter; they were clearly very happy in each other's company. It says much

The market place at Steyr, where Schubert stayed during the summers of 1819, 1823 and 1825

69

for the charm and flexibility of Schubert that he should be able to share in the daily lives of men as diverse as Mayrhofer, Schober and Vogl, and be as happy with all three as they were with him.

Steyr was a beautiful and picturesque town ninety miles west of Vienna, an excellent place for a holiday. Vogl introduced Schubert to the complete circle of his friends; one, Steyr's musical patron, Silvester Baumgartner, promptly commissioned Schubert to write a chamber work for them all to perform. The result was the Piano Quintet known as the Trout because it uses the theme of the song *Die Forelle*. This popular Quintet is the earliest of Schubert's mature chamber works; it is attractive and appealing 'Holiday music for amateurs' as J. A. Westrup puts it; it has not got the weight of Schubert's later chamber music, but it reflects the fun Schubert was having in Steyr, as the sought-after young composer friend of the celebrated singer.

Schubert really enjoyed himself that summer; there were endless outings, music parties, impromptu concerts. He also had a pleasant sufficiency of female company; he wrote to Ferdinand:

At the house where I lodge there are eight girls, nearly all pretty. Plenty to do, you see. The daughter of Herr von Koller, where I and Vogl eat daily, is very pretty, plays the pianoforte well and is going to sing several of my songs.
Please forward the enclosed letter. As you see, I am not quite so faithless as you imagine.

Nothing is known about this letter mentioned by Schubert; but it is clearly for a woman, and since, so far as we know Schubert was still involved with Therese Grob whom Ferdinand lived near and knew well, it could be this letter was intended for her. It is a tantalizing glimpse of an aspect of Schubert's life which he always kept well hidden.

He returned to his room with Mayrhofer in late September and threw himself into his work. October 1819 is one of those specially creative months which occur at intervals throughout his life: during it he composed a piano duet, four settings of Mayrhofer's poems, and two of Goethe's. The commission to write the opera *Die Zauberharfe* for the Theater an der Wien materialized, and he worked hard during that autumn, and the winter of early 1820. He was still waiting for the first performance of *Die Zwillingsbrüder* which was finally given in June 1820. This was his first sizeable work to be performed in public. Schubert's friends packed out the theatre, and overdid their applause at the end in a way which annoyed the rest of the audience. There was a noisy battle until Vogl appeared on the stage and announced: 'Schubert is not present: I thank you in his name.' In fact, Schubert was sitting up in the gallery with Anselm

Johann Wolfgang von Goethe, engraving by Pech

Autograph copy of "Heiden-roslein" (Hedge-rose), a Goethe-song

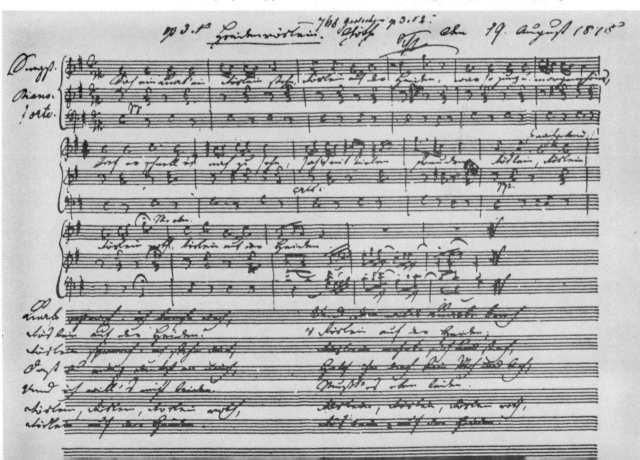

Neues · **Zauberspiel.**

Heute Samstag den 19. August 1820,
wird in dem k. k. priv. Schauspielhause an der Wien
gegeben:

Zum ersten Mahle.

Die Zauberharfe.

Zauberspiel mit Musik in drey Aufzügen.

Musik von Herrn Schubert.

Die neuen Decorationen sind von Herrn Neefe.

Die neuen Maschinerien von Hrn. Roller.

Das neue Costume von Hrn. Lucca Piazza.

Personen:

Arnulf, Graf von Montabor	Hr. Rüger.
Melinde, Arnulfs Gemahlinn	Mad. Gottdank.
Ida von Brabant, Arnulfs Nichte	Mlle. Botta.
Folko, der Adler)	Hr. Heurteur.
Ryno, der Bär) Ritter der Tafelrunde	Hr. Spiseder.
Ulf, der Delphin)	Hr. Demmer.
Sauville,)	Hr. Hann.
Marin,) Brabantische Ritter	Hr. Leeb.
Tirecour)	Hr. Stadelmeyer.
Palmerin, ein Troubadour	Hr. Schimon.
Sutur, Fauergeist	Hr. Küstner.
Ritter, Damen, Pagen, Troubadours, Genien.	
Larven, Wache Volk.	

Freybillete sind ungültig.

Lose zur Lotterie dieses Theaters sind in der Kanzley desselben während den gewöhnlichen Amtsstunden, und Abends an der Kasse zu haben.

Der Anfang ist um 7 Uhr.

Announcement of "Die Zauberharfe" (The Magic Harp)

Johann Michael Vogl

Hüttenbrenner, and had refused to exchange his old frock coat for Anselm's evening tail coat in order to take a curtain call. After the performance he and his friends went to Lenkay's wine shop, a favourite haunt near St Stephen's Cathedral, where they drank Nessmüller (a cheap Hungarian wine) to his success. But the reviews, like the one already quoted, were lukewarm:

Little true tunefulness is to be found, whereas hardly any repose is to be met with in confused and surcharged instrumentation, anxious striving after originality and continual modulation.

Schubert continued to be in the public eye that summer: in August there was a performance of *Die Zauberharfe*, described on the playbills as 'A New Magic Play with Music in Three Acts.' It was under-rehearsed — according to one acid report: 'Nobody knew his part; the prompter was always heard first.' Some of the reviews were bad, deriding the play itself and describing the music as 'thin, insipid and stale in taste'. The Leipzig *Musikalische Zeitung* said:

The score shows talent here and there; but on the whole it lacks technical resource and wants the grasp which old experience can give; most of it is much too long, ineffective and fatiguing, The harmonic progressions are too harsh, the orchestration redundant, the choruses dull and feeble.

But the Vienna '*Conversationsblatt*' wrote: 'What a pity that Schubert's wonderfully beautiful music has not found a worthier subject . . .' and pointed out how poorly the singers had realized the composer's aims. Eight performances only were given before *Die Zauberharfe* returned to permanent obscurity.

There is a poem extant which Schubert wrote in September 1820. It is about divine detachment, and is called *The Spirit of the World*:

Leave them but in their concert,
Tossed on stormy brine:
Though their boat be insecure,
Thus they are still mine.

Thus the spirit of the world
Spake: let them but chase
After dark and far-off goals,
And with wrangling fill their days;

Yet no harm it be for them
Short of truth to fall:
Frail and human is their world,
Godlike understand I all.

Bogner's coffeehouse, much patronised by Beethoven as well as Schubert

Schubert himself needed a modicum of this detachment during the last months of 1820 — not only were his operas unsuccessful, but his old love, Therese, married her master-baker, Johann Bergmann, on 21 November. As usual there are no contemporary diaries or letters to clarify Schubert's own reactions to this event, but it seems, for want of evidence to the contrary, that Therese Grob meant a great deal to Schubert.

In early December Schubert wrote the String Quartet movement in C minor, the *Quartettsatz*, which in every way was a breakthrough in his chamber music as *Gretchen am Spinnrade* had been amongst his songs; he moved suddenly into a new and uniquely Schubertian world. The *Quartettsatz* is unorthodox, original, powerful, full of strange brooding harmonies. There is no customary recapitulation after the veiled development; instead, to quote Alfred Einstein: 'the beginning of the movement reappears towards the end, as if to destroy its rapturous ecstasy and quench its brilliance'. The despairing emotional feel of this music was perhaps a reflection of Schubert's own state of mind at the time. He began to compose a second movement, a rich and tragic *Andante* in A flat major, but never finished it. Had he completed this quartet it would have undoubtedly been a masterpiece.

Schubert's C minor quartet

Chapter 6

Friends and Schubertiads

'Some firm instinct, true and unerring, told Schubert that he was capable, as no man before him, of fixing in music the cry, the emotion of the human heart.' — M. J. E. Brown

The year 1820 had been important for Schubert, with his publicly performed opera, his breakthrough in his chamber music, and finally, with the new and growing habit amongst his friends of holding *Schubertiads*, gatherings and parties where only music by Schubert — songs, dances etc. — was played. The Sonnleithners, the Spauns, the Schobers and others all held Schubertiads and these helped in their small way to spread Schubert's fame. Pressure was put on Schubert, the least business-like of men, to arrange publication of some of his songs. Spaun had already tried, fruitlessly, to bring this about; it was Leopold Sonnleithner who finally succeeded. He describes how he helped Schubert:

. . . suddenly Schubert's name was talked of in all the musical circles and people were asking why his songs were not published. — Meanwhile, through a personal friend of Schubert's (Herr Josef Hüttenbrenner), I had come better acquainted with the former's conditions of life and had discovered that his financial situation was far from satisfactory. We resolved, therefore, to look for a publisher for his works, a task for which Schubert himself, with his naive simplicity, was quite unsuited. I offered the *Erlkönig* to the art dealers Tobias Haslinger and Anton Diabelli; but both refused to publish it (even without fee) as they expected no financial success because the composer was unknown and because of the difficulty of the pianoforte accompaniment. Hurt by this refusal, we decided ourselves to arrange its publication for Schubert's benefit. I, Hüttenbrenner and 2 other art-lovers combined to meet the costs of the first volume out of our own pockets and, in February 1821, we had the *Erlkönig* engraved. When my father announced, at one of our soirées, that the *Erlkönig* was available, almost 100 copies were bought that same evening by those present and the expenses of the 2nd volume were covered. So we had the first 12 works engraved at out own expense and sold on commission at Anton Diabelli's. From the abundant proceeds we paid Schubert's debts, namely his rent, his shoemaker's and tailor's accounts and his debts at the tavern and the coffee-house, and handed over to him, in addition, a considerable sum in cash; unfortunately some guardianship, such as this, was necessary, for he had no idea of domestic economy and was often led by his tavern friends (mostly painters or poets and only a few musicians) into useless expenditure from which the others benefited more than he did himself.

This successful venture with Diabelli's acting as agents encouraged the firm to publish further works themselves; songs, part songs and dances. From this point onwards publication in Vienna of various works proceeded frequently until Schubert's death; by then he was waiting for the publication of Opus 100. Even so, only a tiny proportion of his compositions was published during his lifetime.

Early in 1821 Schubert moved out of Mayrhofer's lodgings into another house nearby. His life was dense with activity at this period, with Schubertiads, evenings in inns with his ever-widening circle of friends, evenings of semi-public performances of earlier works. His composing was only interrupted by the after-effects of his night-life; he wrote early in 1821 to Ferdinand: 'As I was seedy

'Party Game of Schubertians at Atzenbrugg' — a water-colour by Leopold Kupelwieser. Schubert is seated at the fortepiano with Kupelwieser leaning on the instrument: taking shelter underneath is the artist's dog, Drago

today on account of yesterday's dissipations [at Schober's] I did no more work on the Offertory and it is therefore not ready . . .'

Schubert's circle of friends was very much of his own choosing; his delight in the company of those he liked, his discinclinátion to pay court to men of influence, his dislike of and impatience with bores or pretentious people, remained constant throughout his life. Whenever a newcomer was introduced into the group, Schubert was in the habit of asking *Kann er was?* (Can he do anything? or, more colloquially, What's his line?) and this turned into a nickname, 'Canevas' for Schubert. (His other nickname was *Schwammerl*, Tubby, literally 'little mushroom'.)

Schubert's nature and way of life sometimes made him careless of other people's feelings. For example, although Leopold Sonnleithner worked tirelessly on his behalf arranging concerts and publications, he had to write plaintively to one of Schubert's intimates (Josef Hüttenbrenner) begging him to make sure Schubert came to a rehearsal of his songs before a concert. Sonnleithner adds:

Indeed I am surprised that Schubert never appears at our house at all, although I urgently need to speak to him about his *Erlkönig* and other matters.

One feels a little sorry for Sonnleithner, whose memoirs have an air of the solemn bore, a type of person Schubert avoided if he could. But Sonnleithner had reason to be a little aggrieved that Schubert neglected him.

Early in March there had been an important concert held in the Sonnleithners' house. Amongst works by Mozart and Rossini were three of Schubert's, a first performance of the male quartet *Das Dörfchen* (The Little Village), Vogl singing *Erlkönig* and an octet for male voices. According to Hüttenbrenner's recollections, Schubert had been too shy to accompany the singers on the new Graf grand fortepiano; instead he turned the pages. This concert received a certain amount of critical notice in the newspapers; indeed, Schubert's name was frequently in the Vienna newspapers at this period, so much so that Spaun wrote (from Linz) to Schober: 'As regards Schubert, I have to look to the newspapers for the best information about his doings.'

1821 was one of Schubert's good years: remarkably free of problems, unhappiness or other shadows. Publication and critical acclaim were on the increase; and two operas actually performed (even if unsuccessfully) gave Schubert's name a cachet amongst the Viennese. They liked his songs and his dances. The present was happy; the future seemed rosy.

Morgen Mittwoch den 7. März 1821

wird

in dem k. k. Hoftheater nächst dem Kärnthnerthore

mit hoher Bewilligung,

eine große musikalische Akademie

mit Declamation und Gemählde = Darstellungen

verbunden, gegeben werden.

Die einzelnen Gegenstände sind folgende:

Erste Abtheilung:

1. Die Ouverture des Schauspiels: Die Templer auf Cypern.
2. Ein Tableau: Die von Abraham verstoßene Hagar, nach Vandyck, dargestellt von Dlle. Hruschka, k. k. Hofschauspielerinn, Mad. Vogel, k. k. Hofopernsinn, Hrn. Vogl, k. k. Hofoperisten, Dlle. Kraft d. ält., Dlle. Pichler, Herren Pfeiffer, Segatta, Roßi und anderen Mitgliedern des Balletcorps.
3. Eine Arie von Mozart, gesungen von Dlle Wilh. Schröder.
4. Der erste Satz des zweyten Violinconcertes von L. Spohr, gespielt von Hrn. Leon de St. Lubin, dermaligem Schüler des Hrn. Professors der Violine, Joseph Böhm.
5. Der kleine Gernegroß, ein Gedicht von Langbein, vorgetragen von Mad. Wilhelmine Korn, k. k. Hofschauspielerinn.
6. Das Dörfchen, ein Gedicht von Bürger, für zwey Tenor = und zwey Baßstimmen gesetzt von Hrn Franz Schubert, vorgetragen von den Herren Götz und Barth, in Diensten Sr. Durchlaucht des regierenden Herrn Fürsten von Schwarzenberg, und den Herren Nejebse und Umlauf.
7. Variationen für das Pianoforte, componirt von Hrn. Hugo Worzizek, auf zwey Instrumenten gespielt von den zwey Dlles Schadt.
8. Ein Tableau: Sokrates vor seinen Richtern, nach Füger, dargestellt von dem Hrn. Aichinger Vater und Sohn, Reiperger d. ält., Destefani, Rossi, Jos Kohlnberg, Pfeiffer, Wiesenbeck, Segatta und anderen Mitgliedern des Balletcorps.

Zweyte Abtheilung:

9. Die Ouverture der Oper die Zauberglocke (la Clochette), von Boieldieu.
10. Eine Arie von Mozart: Da ich einsam vor dir stehe, gesungen von Dlle. Unger, k. k. Hofopernstinn.
11. Die Gräfinn Spastara im Erdbeben von Messina, 1785, ein Gedicht, vorgetragen von Mad. Sophie Schröder, k. k. Hofschauspielerinn.
12. Der Erlkönig, Gedicht von Göthe, in Musik gesetzt von Franz Schubert, vorgetragen von Hrn. Vogl, k. k. Hofoperisten, auf dem Pianoforte begleitet von Hrn. Anselm Hüttenbrenner.
13. Adagio und Rondo für das Violoncell von Bernhard Romberg, gespielt von Hrn. Pechaczek.
14. Duett aus der Oper: Riccardo e Zoraide, von Rossini (Invan tu fingi, ingrata), gesungen von den Dlles. Schröder und Unger.
15. Der Gesang der Geister über den Wassern, Gedicht von Göthe, für vier Tenor = und vier Baßstimmen gesetzt von Hrn Franz Schubert, vorgetragen von den Herren Götz, Barth, Nejebse, Umlauf, Weinkopf, Fruhwald und zwey Chorsängern.
16. Ein Tableau: Aurora, nach Guido Reni, dargestellt von Hrn. Taglioni, erstem Tänzer der k. k. Hoftheater, und den Dlles. Neuwirth, Mayer, Krepatz, Kreiner, Wittwer, Eisele, Pichler, Kraft d. ält., Fanny Eßler und anderen Mitgliedern des Balletcorps.

Herr Kapellmeister Gyrowetz hat die Leitung dieser Akademie, und Herr Philipp von Stubenrauch die Anordnung der Tableaur übernommen.

Die Einnahme wird von der Gesellschaft adeliger Frauen zur Beförderung ihrer wohlthätigen Zwecke verwendet.

Sämmtlichen Personen, welche mit der menschenfreundlichsten Bereitwilligkeit ihre Talente und Bemühungen gewidmet haben, wird hiermit der verbindlichste Dank abgestattet.

Die Eintrittspreise sind wie gewöhnlich. Die Freybilletten sind ohne Ausnahme ungültig.

Die gesperrten Sitze sind an der k. k. Hoftheater = Casse, die Logen aber bey der Frau Therese Landgräfinn von Fürstenberg, geb. Fürstinn von Schwarzenberg, in der Himmelpfortgasse im Fürstenbergischen Hause Nro. 952. im 2. Stock zu haben.

Der Anfang ist um 7 Uhr.

Program for Schubert concert in March 1821

Ochsenburg Castle at Atzenbrugg,
where Schubert and Schober began
writing the opera *Alfonso and Estrella*

The house at Atzenbrugg

Schubert spent much of that year in Schober's company. They took two holidays together that summer — the first was in July at Atzenbrugg, 20 miles to the north-west of Vienna. Schober's uncle managed a large estate there and every year a small castle was put at Schober's disposal, which he filled with his friends for what they called the 'Atzenbrugg Feasts'. There were excursions, dancing, singing, charades and much eating and drinking. Schubert's first visit had been the year before, in 1820, and this second visit in 1821 was recorded by a painter, Leopold Kupelwieser, who was one of the guests. Kupelwieser, who later became a close friend of both Schubert and Schober, drew separate portraits of them as well as painting two vivid watercolours of the whole group, one of an excursion and the other a game of charades.

In August, back in Vienna, Schubert began work on a new symphony in E, but this, like the D major before it, was never finished although copious sketches exist. Perhaps he shelved it for a new project: an opera, *Alfonso und Estrella*, with Schober as librettist. In order to concentrate on the opera, the two friends left the distractions of Vienna and went back to Atzenbrugg, and then on to St Pölten, where Schober had an uncle who was its Bishop. Schober later wrote a letter to Spaun describing their time there. (Spaun had just left Vienna to live and work at Linz, and was sadly missed by his friends.) Schober says there 'were balls and concerts at St Pölten — in spite of which we worked hard, especially Schubert, who has done nearly two acts, while I am on the last. I only wished you had been there to hear the glorious tunes as they arose: it is wonderful how once again he poured forth rich and teeming ideas. Our room at St Pölten was particularly snug: the twin beds, a sofa next to the warm stove, and a fortepiano made it all very domestic and cosy. In the evenings we always compared notes on what we had done during the day, then sent for beer, smoked our pipes and read, or else Sophie and Nettel [Schober's sister and her friend] came across and there was singing. There were a couple of Schubertiads at the Bishop's, and one at Baroness Münk's, of whom I am quite fond, where a Princess, two Countesses and three Baronesses were present, all most generously ecstatic . . .'

Schubert also wrote a brief note to Spaun on the other side of the sheet, in which he mentions the opera, and says: 'We have great hopes of it'. He then adds: 'The Kärntnertor and Wieden Theatres are actually leased to Barbaja, and he takes over in December'. Domenico Barbaja ran the opera houses at Milan and Naples too; in mentioning his name, Schubert must have known that Barbaja's policy of mounting mainly operas by Italians augured ill for *Alfonso und Estrella*. Soon after Barbaja's arrival several of the best known Viennese singers, Vogl included, left the Court opera in protest.

'Excursion of the Schubertians' from Atzenbrugg to Aumühl. Watercolour by Leopold Kupelwieser, painted in 1820. Schubert is on the far left, with the artist

With Vogl no longer in an influential position, Schubert's chances of succeeding with his opera decreased even more. The fact that Schubert and Schober had embarked on this major project uncommissioned was significant; it was a courageous gesture, typical of the new generation of 'romantic' composers who no longer necessarily wrote to order. He and Schober had deliberately chosen a fashionable theme, often used in contemporary operas, of two lovers who meet in very complicated circumstances, fall in love at first sight, are kept apart by plots of political vengeance and conspiracy, and are finally united — a typical plot of Italian *opera semi-seria*. *Alfonso* is the only 'grand' opera Schubert wrote — all his others have some spoken dialogue. In *Alfonso* he was determined to equal the Italians on their own ground and did not hesitate to imitate the Italian manner. Though the whole opera is uneven, there are some fine moments; Alfred Einstein holds that: 'Adolfo's [the villain] passionately sombre courtship scene, with its powerfully rhythmic orchestral accompaniment, could well have been written by Verdi and a mature Verdi at that'. The opera is, alas, rarely performed.

Schubert had moved into Schober's Vienna apartment in September 1821, the better to work on *Alfonso*, which they finished in February 1822. Just at this time one of the great composers of German opera, Karl Maria von Weber, came to the city to conduct his famous work *Der Freischütz*, a delightful 'magic' opera which Schubert and his friends greatly admired. Indeed, after one of the performances copies of an adulatory poem, written by Schober in praise of Weber, were scattered from the gallery. Clearly Schubert and Schober hoped that Weber would help them promote their new

KEY TO THE PICTURE " A SCHUBERT EVENING," BY MORITZ VON SCHWIND

2. Josef Witteczek 3. Franz Lachner 4. Ignaz Lachner 10. Karl von Schönstein 11. Benedikt Randhartinger 12. Josef von Gahy 14. Johann Michael Vogl 17. SCHUBERT 18. Josef von Spaun 19. Franz von Hartmann 20. Anton von Spaun 22. Kunigunde Vogl 24. Josef Kenner 25. Marie Ottenwalt 27. Moritz von Schwind 28. Anna Hönig 29. August Wilhelm Rieder 30. Leopold Kupelwieser 31. Therese Hönig 32. Anton Dietrich 33. Franz von Schober 36. Franz Grillparzer 37. Justina von Bruchmann 38. Eduard von Bauernfeld 40. Johann Chrisostomus Senn 41. Johann Mayrhofer.

In this sepia drawing, which dates from 1868, the artist is not attempting to portray a single event, but to provide a record of friends and others who had a part to play in the life of the composer. The portrait on the wall is that of Countess Karoline Esterházy, painted by Josef Teltscher.

Detail from the picture "A Schubert Evening"

First page of the first movement of the Symphony No. 1

Portion of the score for the Great C major Symphony

opera. In fact, when it came to the point, Weber withdrew his offer of help because Schubert, with his incurable bluntness, offended him by saying he did not like Weber's latest opera, *Euryanthe*, nearly as much as *Der Freischütz*.

The year 1822 had begun well as far as Schubert's public reputation was concerned, because the Vienna *Musikalische Zeitung* published the first detailed criticism of some of Schubert's songs. It was a sensitive and enthusiastic critique, ending with the statement:

we believe we have done enough to draw our readers' attention to the production of this eminent talent and thus to have rendered an agreeable service to all lovers of truly expressive song.

During the latter part of 1821 and the early months of 1822 Schubert had written little else while concentrating on *Alfonso und Estrella*. When it was finished there followed a fairly unproductive spring and summer; but in September his creative energy returned in full force. He now finished the Mass in A flat which he had started composing three years before. He then began to sketch a new symphony, scoring the first two movements during October; he then set this symphony aside in November and never returned to it. The world knows it as his Unfinished Symphony, one of the best loved symphonies of all time.

Some clarification is needed about the number, and the numbering, of Schubert's symphonies. He wrote, or began to write, ten in all (or eleven if one accepts that the so-called *Gmunden-Gastein* of 1825 ever existed: since it is completely lost and the evidence for its creation is fragmentary, it probably did not).

1. the D major, 1813
2. the B flat major 1814-15
3. the D major, 1815
4. the C minor (The Tragic), 1816
5. the B flat major, 1816
6. the C major (The Little), 1817-18
7. sketches of the D major, 1818
8. full length sketches of the E flat major, 1821
9. 'Unfinished' symphony in B minor, 1822
10. the C major (The Great) completed in 1828

But the numbers of the last two symphonies have been confused over the years because of the existence of the sketches, and the last symphony is commonly known as the Ninth.

Schubert's Unfinished Symphony is so popular and so familiar that it is hard to detach oneself from it in order to judge it objectively. Perhaps it is because of this that M. J. E. Brown has felt:

One feels that the manifold wonders of the symphony, whose music speaks so directly to the heart, have not received their full historical and scholastic acclaim . . . The intimate tone and strongly subjective emotions of his symphony were new in music, and the symmetry and formal beauty which enshrines this personal feeling cannot be too highly praised.

Why did Schubert leave this magnificent symphony unfinished? Many explanations have been given: that he tried to, but could not match the first two incomparable movements; that he intended it to be only that length; that he in fact did write the final two movements but that these were lost by the notorious Hüttenbrenners. They possessed the symphony for forty years; Schubert gave the original manuscript to Anselm in Graz in October 1823, and there it remained in the minute book of the Graz Musikverein, unknown to the musical world until Josef Hüttenbrenner mentioned it in a letter dated 8 March 1860:

The manuscript of the closing bars of the Unfinished Symphony

(Anselm) possesses a treasure in Schubert's B minor symphony, which we rank with his great C major symphony . . . and with all the symphonies of Beethoven — only it is unfinished . . .'

It was finally prised out of the clutches of old Anselm in 1865, and was first performed in Vienna in December 1865, forty-three years after it was written. It is now the most frequently performed of all Schubert's works: 'the unfinished symphony . . . that incomparable song of sorrow we wrong every time we call it ''unfinished'' ' said Einstein.

Schubert kept the sketches of the two completed movements, and of a third, incomplete, Scherzo, obviously meaning to return one day to work on the rest of the symphony — he did, after all, complete his Mass in A begun three years before. Perhaps the main reason why he set the B minor symphony aside was because he had begun a new work. In November he composed his beautiful piano Fantasia in C major, now known as The Wanderer Fantasia. This massive work contains new, ornate piano techniques; it is full of vigour and exuberance and a sense of new directions. The composer Robert Schumann wrote of it in August 1828 — Schubert was still alive —

Schubert would like, in this work, to condense the whole orchestra into two hands, and the enthusiastic beginning is a seraphic hymn to the God-head; you see angels; the Adagio is a gentle meditation on life and takes the veil from off it; then fugues thunder forth a song of endless humanity and music.

Chapter 7

Turning Points

'Furthermore in Schubert there slumbered a dual nature. The Austrian element, uncouth and sensual, revealed itself both in his life and in his art.' —Eduard von Bauernfeld

1822 was a watershed year in Schubert's life; until then his prospects looked hopeful in every way. He had been in the public eye long enough for his music to become better known, his new grand opera had every chance of being performed; his finances were adequate though precarious. He was sought after but as ever only mixed with those he liked. There is a rueful letter from one of his old seminary friends, Anton Holzapfel, to another, Albert Stadler:

> Vienna, 22nd February 1822
>
> . . . Schubert, as they say, made *bruit*, and he will likewise, as they say, make his *sort*. I rarely see him, nor do we hit it off very well, his world being a very different one, as it should be. His somewhat gruff manner stands him in very good stead and will make a strong man and a ripe artist of him; he will be worthy of art . . . Schubert is working at an opera, the words of which are by Schober, a work at which they are said to have both laboured together in mutual understanding.

Schubert's 'gruff manner' was his protection; one of his close friends, Bauernfeld said that

> he suffered from a genuine dread of commonplace and boring people, of philistines, whether from the upper or middle classes, of the people, that is, who are usually known as 'educated'; and Goethe's outcry:
>
> *Lieber will ich schlechter werden,*
> *Als mich ennuyieren!*
> [I would rather die than be bored]
>
> was and remained his motto, as it did ours. Among commonplace people he felt lonely and depressed, was generally silent and apt to become ill-humoured as well, no matter how much attention was paid to this man of rising fame. So it was no wonder if at table he sometimes drank himself into a state of thorough-going tipsiness and then tried to free himself from his oppressive environment by using some coarse expression, which made people shrink away from him in horror.

84

Moritz von Schwind

Leopold Kupelwieser

Schubert's circle of friends were doubtless arrogant to outsiders; they were all young, talented, and felt themselves on the threshold of great achievements. The group had grown; besides the charming painter Leopold Kupelwieser (1796-1862) there was a significant new addition in the beautiful eighteen year old Moritz von Schwind, whom Spaun had introduced to Schubert the year before. Schwind's enthusiasm and brilliance — he could compose almost as well as he could draw and paint — promptly endeared him to Schubert, as did his motto: 'One should take a spoonful of music a day'. Schwind (1804-71) lived to become one of Germany's most distinguished painters and his many pictures of Schubert are amongst the most valuable of Schubertiana.

At that time Schwind lived in a famous Viennese house, the 'Moonshine House' with his mother and sisters, where a regular salon was held; Schubert and Schober were frequent visitors. There is no doubt that Schubert's friends were the most brilliant and interesting of Vienna's artists and intellectuals; they sought him out and were immediately attracted to him. There is no evidence whatever that these men were homosexual; as far as one can tell they were all firmly heterosexual and most of them, including the philandering Schober, later were married. But their affection for each other was warmly demonstrative, and they spent a large part of every day in each other's company.

Josef von Spaun, far away in Linz, pined for the circle of friends, and for their Schubertiads together. He wrote to Schober:

On the whole I am well content, only nothing can make me forget the happy, sociable hours I spent with you all, and which Schubert so often beautified; I fear they will never return so happily for me.

It is poignant that what Spaun misses most of all, he says, is the sound of Schubert's music. He never hears any in Linz.

For most of 1822, Schubert still lived with Schober, and it is clear that some of the accusations of Schober's bad influence were beginning to have substance. One serious result was an estrangement (luckily temporary) with Michael Vogl, who did not approve of Schober's ideas or his way of living, and in addition disliked the new opera *Alfonso und Estrella* and refused to use what influence he still had to bring about a performance in Vienna. A letter dated July 1822 written by Spaun's brother Anton describes the situation:

Vogl is very much embittered against Schober, for whose sake Schubert behaved most ungratefully towards Vogl and who makes the fullest use of Schubert in order to extricate himself from financial embarrassments and to defray the expenditure which has already exhausted the greater part of his mother's fortune. . . Vogl also says Schober's opera is bad and a perfect failure, and that altogether Schubert is quite on the wrong road . . .

The turning point in Schubert's life occurred in the late summer of 1822, when he contracted syphilis. All his friends put this down to Schober's bad influence; Josef Kenner, a Seminary friend who knew both men fairly well, has left a very interesting analysis of their characters (written, though, in 1858, long after the event).

Schubert's genius subsequently attracted, among other friends, the heart of a seductive amiable and brilliant young man, endowed with the noblest talents, whose extraordinary gifts would have been so worthy of a moral foundation and would have richly repaid a stricter schooling than the one he unfortunately had. But shunning so much effort as unworthy of genius and summarily rejecting such fetters as a form of prejudice and restriction, while at the same time arguing with brilliant and ingratiatingly persuasive power, this scintillating individuality, as I was told later, won a lasting and pernicious influence over Schubert's honest susceptibility. If this was not apparent in his work it was all the more so in his life. Anyone who knew Schubert knows how he was made of two natures, foreign to each other, how powerfully the craving for pleasure dragged his soul down to the slough of moral degradation, and how highly he valued the utterances of friends he respected, and so will find his surrender to the false prophet, who embellished sensuality in such a flattering manner, all the more understandable. But more hardened characters than he were seduced, for longer or shorter periods, by the devilish attraction of associating with the apparently warm but inwardly merely vain being into worshipping him as an idol.

This intimation seemed to me indispensable for the biographer's grasp of the subject, for it concerns an episode in Schubert's life which only too probably caused his premature death and certainly hastened it.

Kenner believed with a hindsight, perhaps over-severe, that the whole Schober family possessed 'a deep moral depravity'; Schober himself

devised a philosophical system for his own reassurance and to justify himself in the eyes of the world as well as to provide a basis for his aesthetic oracle, about which he was probably as hazy as any of his disciples; nevertheless he found the mysticism of sensuality sufficiently elastic for his own freedom of movement; and so did his pupils. The need for love and friendship emerged with such egotism and jealousy that to his adherents he alone was all, not only prophet, but God himself and apart from his oracles he was willing to tolerate no other religion, no morals, no restraint.

Kenner points out that 'right-thinking' people soon saw through Schober. It is true that after Schubert's death the others — Spaun (who never liked him much), Schwind and Bauernfeld — all grew away from him, and that Schober was the kind of man who is

Schubert in 1821: a
sketch by Kupelwieser

scintillating in youth but rather pathetic and immature in middle
and old age.

Whatever the full extent of Schober's 'equivocal moral
behaviour', he certainly influenced Schubert to lead a life which
brought about his infection. No cure for syphilis then existed, and
doctors were unclear about the development of its various stages.

Syphilis progresses through three stages: the primary, with
chancre in the part affected two to three weeks after infection; the
secondary, one to two months after infection, with rashes, sore
throat, general enlargement of the glands, anaemia and fever.
(These two stages are infectious.) The final stage could occur two to
ten years after infection; the bones, muscles and brain become
affected, and general paralysis ensues. In Schubert's case, of course,
the disease never reached the third stage; it was typhoid fever that
killed him, but his body was weakened by the symptoms of the
second stage. This unpleasant and serious disease which he alone of
his circle had contracted, would definitely have cut short his life
and made his last years a horror. Given his circumstances, it was
perhaps lucky he died young.

Schubert himself would of course have been unaware then of the
full relentless progress of the disease, but he realized its seriousness
and this knowledge seems to have strengthened his creative drive.
During the first onset of his illness he was busy with his Unfinished
Symphony and the Wanderer Fantasia. In his last six years he
rarely let bad health or depression affect the quantity of music he
wrote. It affected its quality, however: it may be a truism to say that
suffering refines the mind and heart — in Schubert's case there are
the many masterpieces of his last years as evidence.

With the onset of his disease he moved out of Schober's house
and returned to his family, where he lived for the next six months.
He was in close touch with his friends and attended Schubertiads
when he could. A letter he wrote to Spaun in December describes
how upset he was by 'the miserable affair of the opera' — *Alfonso*
was not being taken up by the theatre management in Vienna.
Schubert tells Spaun that he and Vogl are friends again. He ends
his letter:

Our companionship in Vienna is quite agreeable now. We hold readings at
Schober's three times a week as well as a Schubertiad . . . And now, dear
Spaun, farewell. Do write to me soon at length, so as to mitigate somewhat
the gaping void your absence will always make for me.

These reading parties which had started up were of the greatest
value to Schubert: he was always looking for new poetry to set, and
his friends' informed tastes introduced him to the latest publications and translations. He had become very much a 'modern'

composer, setting mainly contemporary poetry, often to music which his critics found harsh, difficult and remote. His friends, however, with their consistent interest, understanding and enthusiasm, encouraged him to continue developing his art; in fact, Schubert's friends played an unusually important role in his creative life.

By them Schubert was introduced to a new poet, Friedrich Rückert, and composed a magnificent group of songs in February to four of his poems. *Du Bist die Ruh* (You are rest and peace) is a masterpiece which goes straight to the heart of most listeners. It is a love song with a sad undertone; not only the request

> *Drive other griefs*
> *Out of my breast.*
> *Let my heart be full*
> *Of your joy*

but the piano part suggests that the singer has lived through some tragic experience. There is no doubt that, with some obvious exceptions — *An die Musik* is one — the better the poem, the better the song Schubert wrote. But even when the poem was good, he often made changes to suit its fusion with music. In *Du Bist die Ruh* he reorganized the very shape of the poem by changing the five brief

'A Family at Play' — a painting very much in the Biedermeier style by Moritz von Schwind

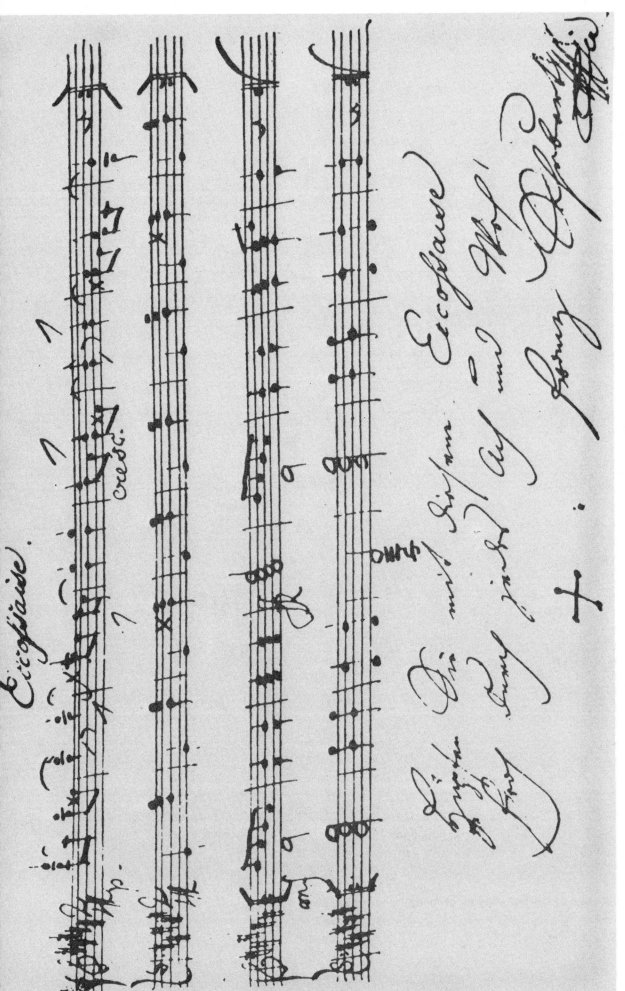

An ecossaise for piano copied by Schubert into the album of a friend, 1823

First page of the fair copy of *Erlkonig*

stanzas into three musical strophes — to balance the song the last stanza had to be repeated. ('Why', Tennyson is reported to have growled, 'do these damned musicians make me say a thing twice when I said it only once?') In this case Schubert's changes are fully justified; not only is the melody itself unforgettable, but Rückert's fine poem is transformed into something greater than it was before. The melody alone is unforgettable.

It has been said that a successful *Lied* marries the principles of recitative and aria. In an oratorio, for instance, the narrative and the emotions aroused by it are usually presented alternately; in a *Lied* they go together. Like an aria, operatic or otherwise, a *Lied* can bear a certain amount of word repetition when it helps the musical form and adds to the total impact; but a *Lied* is less static than an aria because it also contains the continuity, the telling of the story, as well as the emotional reaction.

Not all good poetry lends itself to composition; the imagery must not be too intense or bold, or it can destroy the balance between word sense and melodic line; the words and thoughts must be simple enough to be followed when sung; the poem must be as terse as possible, and finally it must leave much to the composer's imagination, so that the music has work to do. In Schubert's case it was the simple, terse, deeply-felt poem which most stimulated him.

Schubert was ill on and off all the winter of 1822-23, and often confined to the house. Several business letters survive from this period; obviously when he was well he conducted his Viennese publishing affairs in person. Not that he was ever systematic, nor did he possess any business acumen. Leopold Sonnleithner describes the mistakes he made after the first successful publications had been arranged of *Erlkönig* and other songs:

If his affairs had continued like this, Schubert would have received great profit from his works and would have remained the owner of them. But behind our backs, Diabelli offered him 800 fl. A.C. [Austrian Currency] for the plates and copyright of the first 12 works; this sum induced Schubert into accepting the offer and then it was all over with his freedom. For these twelve works he got about 2000 fl. A.C. in all, which makes an average of 166 fl. for each work, a fee he never attained again later. This really rather ungrateful behaviour on Schubert's part did not estrange him from us in any way; we regretted his weakness but continued to promote the performance and furtherance of his works.

Schubert, in company with many others, hated the business side of his art; all he needed was enough cash to meet his modest wants, and if there was any over he spent it on his friends. For men to whom success meant financial and social status Schubert had little patience, however well-meant their concern for him was. This carelessness was galling to Sonnleithner, who loved Schubert's music and felt it could bring him fame and gain.

After a winter suffering from the secondary stage of syphilis, Schubert wrote a poem in May 1823 which evokes with some power the despair he felt at his painful condition.

My Prayer

With a holy zeal I yearn
Life in fairer worlds to learn;
  Would this gloomy earth might seem
  Filled with love's almighty dream.

Sorrow's child, almighty Lord,
Grant Thy bounty for reward.
  For redemption from above
  Send a ray of endless love.

See, abased in dust and mire
Scorched by agonizing fire,
  I in torture go my way
  Nearing doom's destructive day.

Take my life, my flesh and blood,
Plunge it all in Lethe's flood,
  To a purer, stronger state
  Deign me, Great One, to translate.

This poem, though theistic, is not specifically Christian; in the last verse it is not clear what Great One he is invoking. He had moved far away from his strict Catholic upbringing.

Despite the pain and depression he felt at this time, his compositions did not reflect it; he composed a gay and highspirited one-act opera *Die Verschworenen* (The Conspirators) in March and April; and in May, commissioned by the Theater an der Wien, he began a three-act opera, *Fierabras*, to a poor libretto by Josef Kupelwieser (Leopold's brother) which did not inspire Schubert to write his best music. Yet he composed at white heat: the manuscript score of *Fierabras* provides an example of the extraordinary speed at which Schubert could work: in only ten days he wrote 604 of its 1,000 pages. In the midst of all this activity, his illness grew worse and he was admitted for a short spell to the Vienna General Hospital. He spent the summer recuperating away from Vienna; joining Vogl at Steyr for a while, and going also to Linz to stay with Spaun. It was in this year, 1823, that Schubert made his final push for success in opera; his three works, *Die Verschworenen*, *Fierabras* and finally *Rosamunde* all surpass his earlier efforts in quality, but only *Rosamunde* was performed at all — and even then only received two performances. Embittered by his lack of success, Schubert stopped

Schubert in 1825 (*water-colour by Wilhelm August Rieder*)

wasting his time on opera. The reasons for his failure in this are mixed, and reveal much about the musical and social background.

Schubert had poor libretti, but the main reason for his failure lay in the musical scene: opera was so Italian-dominated that composers who wanted to write German operas like *Fidelio* or *Der Freischütz* were up against immense commercial and musical prejudice. Very few romantic German operas were commissioned; even fewer succeeded. The management, the public and the singers did not want them; they wanted Rossini, or light French opera. A letter to Schubert from his friend Anna Milder, the famous soprano, is most illuminating. He had written to her asking her help in getting *Alfonso und Estrella* performed in Berlin; she replied in March 1825:

With regard to your opera *Alfonso und Estrella* it pains me to remark that the libretto does not answer the taste of the people here, who are accustomed to the grand tragic high opera, or the comic opera of the French. You will understand that success here would be impossible.

The same was equally true for Vienna. It is just as well Schubert gave up the struggle to win fame on the operatic stage, and concentrated on what he was good at; the contrast between the tedious *Fierabras* and the song cycle Schubert began work on concurrently in the summer of 1823 could not be greater. The latter is incomparably better; and makes one wonder what Schubert would have made of a really good libretto, a libretto containing characters and situations which were real, credible, and with the pungency of

'*Die schöne Müllerin*' cover design

Wilhelm Müller, librettist of both 'Die schöne Müllerin' and 'Die Winterreise' song cycles

ordinary human life, instead of the usual fashionable pseudo-Gothic farrago he was given. It might have drawn from him the *sustained* dramatic power one feels he possessed but never gave evidence of in his short life.

Wilhelm Müller's poem sequence *Die Schöne Müllerin* (The Fair Maid of the Mill) had everything Schubert needed: a taut, very human story, with subtly suggested characters in a credible setting. Schubert edited the text with his usual confidence by leaving out Müller's prologue and epilogue, and three songs, one from each emotional stage of the cycle: hope, love, and jealousy; he then set the twenty remaining songs as they stood. He had an instinctive knowledge of what made a good *Lied*; it is a pity that he never applied this instinct to the problems of an opera libretto. The sure touch with which he moulded a series of poems to suit his music deserted him when he was confronted by the extended text of an opera.

Müller (1794-1827) who had written these poems two years before, liked his work to be set to music. It was ironical that he never lived to know what Schubert had done for *Die Schöne Müllerin* and, later, for *Winterreise*; he even wrote sadly to a composer friend:

. . . my songs lead but half a life, a paper life of black and white . . . until music breathes life into them, or at least calls it forth and awakens it if it is already dormant in them . . .

Music did indeed 'breathe life into them'. *Die Schöne Müllerin* is a most beautiful and moving work, perfect from first note to last. It tells the story of a young miller who decides to wander — he explains how the very water which turns the millwheel encourages him because it never stops moving. He follows a charming stream which brings him to a mill 'gleaming through the alders'; the stream seems to say *Zur müllerin hin* — away to the maid of the mill — and he accepts his fate and stops there, to work for the miller. He falls in love with the girl, and confides this to the stream, asking it if she loves him. He wants to broadcast the news of his love, and the methods he chooses are vivid and typical of a young country boy: he wants to

Sow it on every newly turned plot
With cress-seed that will soon betray it.

and

I would like to train a young starling
To speak the words loud and clear.

93

Schubert's spectacles which were often to be seen on top of his head

(These circumstantial details obviously delighted Schubert.) The young girl slowly falls in love with the new assistant, they sit cosily by the stream in the tenth song, called *Tränenregen* (Rain of Tears) and the boy gazes at her reflection and her blue eyes, which are the same colour as the forget-me-nots on the bank.

> *And the whole sky seemed*
> *sunk into the stream*
> *and wanted to drag me down*
> *into its depths . . .*
>
> *The tears welled up in my eyes*
> *and the watery mirror was blurred*
> *She said: 'We shall have rain.*
> *Goodbye — I am going home.'*

The next poem is triumphant; the girl has returned his love. He hangs up his lute because his heart is too full to sing any more; it has a green ribbon hanging down, and the girl says: 'I am so fond of green', so the boy gives it to her, to wear in her hair. Green is where hope dwells, he sings. But green is also the colour of jealousy, and in the next song, no. 14, the huntsman arrives and promptly woos and wins the fickle girl. The sixteenth song, *Die Liebe Farbe* (The Beloved Colour) now identifies green as the colour of misery — willows, cypresses, the green turf over a grave. The next song takes this anger further; green is a hateful colour now — and the boy would travel away, but the whole countryside is so full of green. 'I would like to pluck the green leaves from every branch.' The flowers the girl once gave him are withered.

Tears, alas, do not bring back the green of May
nor can they make a dead love bloom again.

The millstream is his only comfort; and in the last song we hear only the millstream, because the young miller has drowned himself in his despair.

Do not look in,
little blue flowers!
You bring such bad dreams to this sleeper.

Die Schöne Müllerin illustrates very clearly the various forms of song Schubert wrote; first, there was the *strophic* song, in which each verse is sung to the same tune to the same accompaniment; the strophic song often has a refrain as well, or recitative between the verses, or is further modified so that each verse contains melodic variations. Then there is the *scenic* type of song, more dramatic, in which there are several quite distinct sections with different key signatures and tempi; and thirdly the 'on-running', 'through-composed' or *durchkomponiert* song, in which the uniform accompaniment forms the basic unity of a song full of ranging moods and ideas receiving different musical treatments. Schubert used all three types consistently throughout his life. The strophic song is the most immediately appealing, and seems the simplest, but in fact is perhaps the hardest to compose: Brahms, for instance, said that a declamatory song (usually on-running) was child's play to compose compared with the devising of a strophic melody which suited every stanza of a poem. *Du Bist die Ruh*, described earlier, is a beautiful example of a strophic song.

Die Schöne Müllerin is another turning point in the history of music — nobody had composed a song cycle like this before. The text and music form an exquisite whole. There has never been a more spontaneous composer than Schubert, and his response to Müller's poems illustrates this to perfection; his music seems so artless, so effortless, so emotionally right. His technical mastery of his medium is unobtrusive but complete.

Chapter 8

Moonshine House

'Pain sharpens the understanding and strengthens the mind; whereas joy seldom troubles about the former and softens the latter and makes it frivolous.' — Schubert (1824)

While Schubert was recuperating at Steyr with Vogl, he wrote Schober this rather subdued letter showing he was aware of the long-term nature of his disease:

14 August 1822

Dear Schober

Although I write rather late, I hope this letter will still find you in Vienna. [Schober was about to go for two years to Breslau, where he intended to become an actor.] I correspond busily with Schäffer [his doctor] and am fairly well. Whether I shall ever quite recover I am inclined to doubt. Here I live very simply in every respect, go for walks regularly, work much at my opera and read Walter Scott.

None of the correspondence with his doctor has survived; if any letters about his disease were found among his papers, someone, probably Ferdinand, destroyed them.

Schubert's quiet summer of recuperation was marked by the towns of Steyr and Linz making him an honorary member of their musical societies. He returned to Vienna in the middle of September, where he resumed his social life as much as his health would permit. The many letters written at this time to Schober in Breslau describe frequent reading parties, Schubertiads etc., but for Schubert these evenings were no longer the same without Schober.

Vienna, 30th November 1823

Dear Schober,

For some time I have been itching to write to you, but I have never managed to do so. You know how it happens.

First of all I must pour out a lament over the condition of our circle as well as all other circumstances; for with the exception of the state of my health, which (thank God) seems to be firmly restored at last, everything goes miserably. Our circle, as indeed I had expected, has lost its central focus without you. Bruchmann, who has returned from his journey, is no longer the same. He seems to bend to the formalities of the world, and by that alone he loses his halo, which in my opinion was due only to his determined disregard of all worldly affairs. Kupelwieser, as presumably you already know, has gone to Rome . . . As for the others, you know better than I . . . what is the good of a lot of quite ordinary students and officials to us? . . . We go on for hours hearing nothing but eternal talk about riding, fencing, horses and hounds. If it is to go on like this, I don't suppose I shall stand it for long among them. —

With my two operas things go very badly, too. Kupelwieser [Josef] has suddenly left the theatre. Weber's '*Euryanthe*' turned out wretchedly and its bad reception was quite justified, in my opinion. These circumstances . . . leave me scarcely any hope for my opera. Besides, it would really not be a great stroke of fortune, as everything is done indescribably badly now.

Vogl is here . . . He is taken up with my songs almost exclusively. He writes out the voice-part himself and, so to speak, lives on it. He is therefore very polite and docile with me. And now let's hear from you. How are you? Have you already appeared before the world's eyes?

Please be sure to give some news of yourself very soon, and still my longing for you to some extent at least by letting me know how you live and what you do. — I have composed nothing since the opera, except a few '*Maid of the Mill*' songs. The '*Mill*' songs will appear in four books, with vignettes by Schwind. —

For the rest, I hope to regain my health, and this recovered treasure will let me forget many a sorrow; only you, dear Schober, I shall never forget, for what you meant to me no one else can mean, alas!

And now keep well and do not forget

> Your eternally affectionate
> friend,
> Franz Schubert.

My address:
Stubentor-Bastei,
No.1187, first floor.

(Since returning to Vienna, he had moved out of his father's house and was living on his own again.) Moritz von Schwind also confirmed that Schubert's health was better, when he wrote just before Christmas to Schober:

Schubert is better and it will not be long before he goes about with his own hair again, which had to be shorn owing to the rash. He wears a very cosy wig. He is much with Vogl . . . The dratted doctor is often with him, too . . .

With these two close friends of Schubert's, Schober and Kupelwieser, abroad for two years, there are many lively letters extant which tell us a great deal about Schubert's life. His health clearly was much better for the moment; one of Schwind's letters describes Schubert's twenty-seventh birthday celebrations on 31 January at

The Hungarian Crown
Inn in the Seilerstätte

the 'Hungarian Crown' inn where everyone became tipsy and
Schubert fell asleep. Ten days after that Schwind wrote again to
Schober, whom he worshipped ('you have ranked me with you and
Schubert, and I could not bear the delight of if'):

Schubert now keeps a fortnight's fast and confinement. He looks much
better and is very bright, very comically hungry and writes quartets and
German dances and variations without number . . . He has given up his
wig and shows a charming cygnet's down.

A week later, Schwind writes again to describe the excellent effects
of a new treatment Schubert was undergoing:

He says that after a few days of the new treatment he felt how his
complaint broke up and everything was different. He still lives one day on
panada [bread boiled to a pulp and flavoured with sugar and spices] and
the next on cutlets, lavishly drinks tea, goes bathing a good deal besides
and is superhumanly industrious. A new Quartet is to be performed at
Schuppanzigh's, who is quite enthusiastic, which is said to have rehearsed
particularly well. He has now long been at work on an Octet, with the
greatest zeal. If you go to see him during the day, he says, 'Hullo, how are
you? — Good!' and goes on writing, whereupon you depart . . .

Ignaz Schuppanzigh, famous as a friend of Beethoven's, was the
leader of an unrivalled string quartet, and the excellent playing of
these men inspired Schubert to compose for them. He had also met
another virtuoso instrumentalist, the clarinettist Count Troyer,
who commissioned the Octet in F major for Strings and wind
instruments. Between January and March 1824 Schubert composed

98

three important works: two String Quartets, in A major and in D minor; and the Octet; and four beautiful settings of poems by Mayrhofer, *Der Sieg* (Victory), *Abendstern* (Evening Star), *Auflösung* (Dissolution) and *Gondelfahrer* (Gondolier); and finally a captivating part song using *Gondelfahrer* for male voice quartet. This is one of Schubert's most popular partsongs, and shows his complete mastery of that form for which the Viennese demand was insatiable.

The A minor quartet, which contains in its andante the familiar *Rosamunde* tune, opens in a mood of powerfully expressive sadness. There are many passages of gaiety and charm, but the overall mood of the quartet is grey, melancholy.

All I have created is born of my understanding of music and my own sorrow: that which is engendered by grief alone seems to please the world least of all.

wrote Schubert in his diary, soon after the first public performance. The only one of his quartets to be published during his lifetime, it was actually the thirteenth of the fifteen he was to compose. A newspaper critic referred to it as his 'first-born' and another said: 'This composition must be heard many times before it can be adequately judged.'

The D minor Quartet, 'Death and the Maiden', is yet another

. . . while Schwind, together with his brothers, lived at the back

Schubert masterpiece; the defiant, restless and passionate mood of the first movement; the theme from the 1817 song *Der Tod und das Mädchen* of the second movement; the savagely insistent scherzo and the finale, which is a 'wild tarantella, carried through with unflagging energy to a tempestuous conclusion' — all these movements have a unity in both mood and theme. J. A. Westrup, whose words have just been quoted, goes on:

The whole quartet is informed by one consistent purpose, and the means by which that purpose is executed are so convincing that no one hearing this work for the first time could ever doubt that Schubert was one of the great masters.

He did not write another quartet for two years.

There are rare and valuable insights into his state of mind at this period. Firstly, he kept a notebook during 1824 which was subsequently lost, but not before passages of it were quoted by Bauernfeld, including the following passionate statement which also tells us much about Schubert the man:

What I hate from the bottom of my heart is that one-sidedness which makes so many wretches believe that only what they happen to be doing is best, everything else being worthless. One kind of beauty should hold a man's enthusiasm all through his life, it is true; but the glow of that enthusiasm should light up everything else.

The other illuminating document is a long letter Schubert wrote to Leopold Kupelwieser in Rome.

Vienna, March 31, 1824

Dear Kupelwieser,

I've been wanting to write to you for some time, but was so busy I hardly knew which way to turn. But now the opportunity has come through Smirsch and at last I can pour out my feelings again to someone. You are indeed so staunch and true. You will surely forgive me many things which others would take amiss. To put it briefly, I feel myself the most unfortunate, the most miserable being in the world. Think of a man whose health will never be right again, and who from despair over the fact makes it worse instead of better; think of a man, I say, whose splendid hopes have come to naught, to whom the happiness of love and friendship offer nothing but acutest pain, whose enthusiasm (at least, the inspiring kind) for the Beautiful threatens to disappear, and ask yourself whether he isn't a miserable, unfortunate fellow?

My peace is gone, my heart is heavy,
I find it never, nevermore . . .

so might I sing every day, since each night when I go to sleep I hope never again to wake, and each morning merely reminds me of the misery of

Portion of Otto Nowak's portrait of Schubert

Title page of Opus 10, Variations on a French Song for piano
four-hands, dedicated to Beethoven

Ludwig van Beethoven: an oil painting by W. J. Mähler, 1815 (*Karajan Collection, Salzburg*)

yesterday. So I should pass my days joyless and friendless, if it weren't for Schwind, who frequently visits me and sheds a light from those dear, departed days.

Our Society (Reading Society), as you probably know by now, being swollen with uncouth crowds for beer-swilling and sausage-eating, has committed suicide, for its dissolution takes place in 2 days, although since your departure I rarely went to it. Leidesdorf, whom I have come to know quite well, is indeed a really profound and good fellow, yet so deeply melancholy, that I am almost afraid I have profited from him in that respect more than I care to do; also, his and my affairs are going badly, so we never have any money. Your brother's opera (he did not do very well to leave the theatre) was pronounced unusable, and accordingly no claim has been made on my music. [This opera was *Die Verschworenen*.] In this way I appear to have composed, once again, two operas for nothing. I have done very little song-writing, but tried my hand at several instrumental things, for I have composed two quartets for violins, viola and 'cello, and an Octet, and want to write another string quartet, on the whole I want to prepare myself like this for grand Symphony.

The latest news in Vienna is that Beethoven is giving a Concert, at which he intends to produce his new Symphony, 3 pieces from the new Mass, and a new Overture. God willing, I also am thinking of giving a similar concert next year. Now I close, so as not to use too much paper, and kiss you a 1000 times. If you would write to me about your own enthusiasms and your life as well, nothing would more greatly please

Your
faithful friend
Frz Schubert.

My address, then, would be c/o Sauer & Leidesdorf, because I am going at the beginning of May to Hungary with Esterházy.

Farewell! Really well!!

Beethoven's concert was on 7 May in the Kärntnertor Theatre, and included the first public performance of the Ninth Symphony. Schubert must have attended this concert. His relationship with Beethoven remains unclarified; it appears he did not know him, yet Vienna was a small city and most people involved in music or the theatre knew each other, if only slightly. It is therefore surprising that Schubert never met Beethoven though he must have caught sight of him many times. He was evidently too shy to approach him directly; he did dedicate a work to him, Variations on a French Song for piano duet, published in 1822, which was said to have pleased the great man so much he said Schubert had 'the divine spark'. Perhaps M. J. E. Brown makes the best statement about the two composers:

It is Schubert's chief glory that he could be contemporary with a dominating figure like Beethoven, without slavishly imitating him.

101

When Schubert visited
Zseliz for the second time
he was offered a room in
this building — a delicate
indication of his advance
up the social ladder

In late May, Schubert left Vienna for his second stay as music
tutor at Zseliz: this time, as a rising young composer, he was lodged
in the castle itself. There are many interesting letters between him and
his family and friends; a stiff one from his father dated late June
urges him to take care of his health in such generalized tones that it
seems Schubert did not tell him of the exact nature of his illness.
Ferdinand certainly knew by this time; he writes a letter to
Schubert in July:

Now, dear Franz, write to me to say how you are (but expressly addressed
to me).

This very much implies that in the family he alone was in his
brother's confidence. Schubert replies promptly to this letter:

I feel more clearly than ever at this moment that you, and you only, are my
truest friend, bound to my soul with every fibre! — Not to let these lines
mislead you into believing that I am not well or cheerful, I hasten to assure
you of the contrary! True, it is no longer that happy time during which
each object seems to us to be surrounded by a youthful aura, but a period
of fateful recognition of a miserable reality, which I endeavour to beautify
as far as possible by my imagination.

Schubert worked hard that summer, both teaching and
composing. For example, he was asked at breakfast time to compose
a quartet of mixed voices; a noted tenor, Baron Schönstein, was
staying as a guest at the time and described the day:

One morning in September 1824, in which year I once again spent some
weeks in Zseliz with my friends, Countess Esterházy invited *Meister*
Schubert during breakfast, which we all took together, to set to music for
our four voices a poem of which she was particularly fond; it was the
above-mentioned 'Gebet'. Schubert read it, smiled inwardly, as he usually

did when something appealed to him, took the book and retired forthwith, in order to compose. In the evening *of the same day* we were already trying through the finished song at the piano from the manuscript. Schubert accompanied it himself. If our joy and delight over the Master's splendid work were already great that evening, these feelings were still further enhanced the next evening, when it was possible to perform the splendid song with greater assurance and certainty from the vocal parts, which had now been written out by Schubert himself, the whole thereby gaining in intelligibility. It is understandable that anyone familiar with this opus and its not exactly small dimensions will feel sceptical of the truth of what I have said, when he realizes, in addition, that Schubert produced this work in barely ten hours. It certainly seems incredible, but it is nevertheless true. After all, Schubert was the man for that kind of thing, this heaven-inspired clairvoyant who, as it were, simply shook his most glorious things out of his sleeve (to use a colloquial expression). The composition was unknown to the public at that time, as it was written for the E. family, and the manuscript was acquired from Schubert on the condition that it was not to be published.

Again, Schubert's speed of composition prompts people to class him as a 'clairvoyant'. It is clear from all accounts that the actual creating of music came wonderfully easily to him, but his phenomenal speed resulted from unusual powers of concentration and application, and not simply from facility.

According to his letters, the four months he spent in Hungary were uneventful. How strong his affection was for his long-standing pupil, Countess Karoline (now aged nineteen) is another of the unsolved questions in Schubert's emotional life; he himself gives only one indication of any special feelings, when he says to Schwind in a letter that he is longing for Vienna 'in spite of a certain attractive star'. Eduard von Bauernfeld, who got to know Schubert well only in the following year, 1825, has no doubts about his feelings:

Countess Karoline
Esterházy

He was, in fact, head over ears in love with one of his pupils, a young Countess Esterházy, to whom he also dedicated one of his most beautiful piano pieces, the Fantasy in F minor for pianoforte duet. In addition to his lessons there, he also visited the Count's home, from time to time, under the aegis of his patron, the singer Vogl, who associated with princes and counts as though he were their equal, swaggered wherever he went and, when he took the gifted composer under his wing, behaved like a mahout who just then had a special rarity from the animal kingdom to exhibit. On such occasions Schubert was quite content to take a back seat, to remain quietly by the side of his adored pupil, and to thrust love's arrow ever deeper into his heart. For the lyric poet, as well as for the composer, an unhappy love affair may have its advantages, provided it is not altogether too unhappy, as it enhances his subjective feelings and stamps the poems and songs, which spring from it, with the colour and tone of purest reality.

(Bauernfeld rather gives himself away in the last sentence: clearly the group of friends indulged in a certain amount of exaggeration to fulfil their image of the 'romantic' artist.) Baron Schönstein also believed the story of Schubert's love for Countess Karoline. In his 1857 memoirs he mentions how Schubert was a frequent visitor to the Esterházy household in Vienna, as a music master; he goes on:

A love affair with a maid-servant, which Schubert started soon after he entered this house [Zseliz], subsequently gave way to a more poetic flame which sprang up in his heart for the younger daughter of the house, Countess Karoline. This flame continued to burn until his death. Karoline had the greatest regard for him and for his talent but she did not return this love; perhaps she had no idea of the degree to which it existed. I say the *degree*, for *that* he loved her must surely have been clear to her from a remark of Schubert's — his only declaration in words. Once, namely, when she reproached Schubert in fun for having dedicated no composition to her, he replied 'What is the point? Everything is dedicated to you anyway'.

Yet Schubert himself wrote to Schober from Zseliz;

Now I sit here alone in the depth of the Hungarian countryside, where I have unfortunately allowed myself to be enticed a second time, without having a single person around with whom I could exchange a sensible word.

This marble fountain known, inevitably, as the Trout fountain, was carved by Josef Müllner and placed in the courtyard of Schubert's birthplace in 1911

Hardly the words of a man in love with someone living in the same house. But whatever his feelings for the Countess Karoline, then or later, the fact remains that he did write some beautiful piano music for her, and in dedicating the Wanderer Fantasia to her, paid her a very great compliment indeed. She was not only pretty, but musical, and Schubert was possibly infatuated rather than in love; he had always realized that his social and financial position, and now his illness, meant that he could not take any affair of the heart seriously.

He returned to Vienna in October, travelling with Baron Schönstein who was irritated that 'the lackadaisical Schubert managed to smash the window at the back of the coach . . . whereby the ghastliest of cold winds was given free play about our ears'. After Schubert's arrival in Vienna Schwind wrote gleefully to Schober:

S. is here, well and divinely frivolous, rejuvenated by delight and pain and a pleasant life.

Schubert remained frivolous until the New Year; he lived a busy social life and hardly composed anything. He was living temporarily with his father again, but spent most of his time with

Schwind. Their cheerful irresponsible relationship is epitomised in this anecdote of Schwind's:

One morning Schwind turned up at Schubert's to take him on an excursion. Schubert hurried to finish his dressing and was rummaging in his chest of drawers for a pair of socks. But, however much he rummaged, every pair turned out to be hopelessly torn to pieces. 'Schwind', said Schubert, with superstitious seriousness, at the end of this forlorn inspection, 'Schwind, now I really do believe that whole ones are not knitted any more'.

Schwind entertained his friends constantly in the Moonshine House; at Christmas, 1824, he gave a special party and prepared a large Christmas tree (then a new habit in Vienna) hung with little drawings and verses for everyone. It is not surprising that Schubert found a room near the Moonshine House, and lodged there from the New Year 1825 for eighteen months. Schwind, delighted with this arrangement, wrote to Schober in February:

Schubert is well and busy again after a certain stagnation. He had recently come to live next door to us, where the alehouse is, in a very pretty room. We meet daily, and as far as I can I share his whole life with him.

This ingenuous remark of Schwind's may help to explain why Schubert's output was lower than usual throughout that period; beautiful songs, but only forty in the two years 1824 and 1825; no chamber or orchestral music after the two quartets and the octet until 1826. Most of his compositions were duets, sonatas and dances for piano. Schubert's life was full of people, and people take up time. He saw all his friends constantly; he often appeared at weekly Schubertiads, accompanying Vogl. These two got to know Sophie Müller, a celebrated actress and singer whom the Viennese idolized; there are frequent entries in Sophie Müller's diary recording their visits:

3 March 1825

After lunch Schubert came and brought a new song, '*The Young Nun*'; later Vogl came, and I sang it to him; it is splendidly composed.

Sophie Müller was an excellent interpreter of Schubert's songs, and was perhaps the inspiration behind such masterpieces for women's voices as *Die Junge Nonne* and, later that year, the exquisite *Delphine*.

The most important addition to Schubert's circle at this time was Eduard von Bauernfeld (1802-90) who had known about Schubert for three years but only now became a close friend of his. Bauernfeld was later to be an eminent German playwright and esteemed man of letters. He has left vivid records of his life with Schubert. When he first met Schubert properly he was studying law, but gave most of his time and attention to poetry and to the translation of an edition of Shakespeare. Bauernfeld describes the meeting and the effect it had on his life.

I was sitting thus in my den, one evening in February 1825, when my boyhood friend, Schwind, brought Schubert to see me, who meanwhile had already become famous or, at least, well known. We were soon on intimate terms with one another. At Schwind's request I had to recite some crazy youthful poems of mine; we then went to the piano, where Schubert sang and we also played duets, and later to an inn till far into the night. The bond was sealed, the three friends remained inseparable from that day on. But others too grouped themselves round us, mostly painters and musicians, a circle of people, with a zest for life and with similar aims and ideas, who shared together their joys and sorrows . . .

. . . How often did we three wander about until the small hours, accompanying one another home — but as we could not bring ourselves to part, it was not uncommon for us all to spend the night together, at one or other's lodgings. We were not very particular about comfort on these occasions! If necessary, friend Moritz would throw himself down on the bare floor boards, wrapped only in a feather coverlet, and once, when I did not have one, he carved Schubert's spectacle case into a pipe for me. In the

Vogl and Schubert —
pencil sketch by Schwind

Eduard von Bauernfeld

matter of property the communistic viewpoint prevailed; hats, boots, neckerchiefs, even coats and certain other articles of clothing too, if they but chanced to fit, were common property; but gradually, through manifold use, as a result of which a certain partiality for the object always ensues, they passed into undisputed private possession. Whoever was flush at the moment paid for the other, or for the others.

Bauernfeld gives a realistic description of what happened at

the so-called 'Schubertiads', with gay and lively companions, when the wine flowed like water, the excellent Vogl treated us to all the wonderful songs and poor Franz Schubert had to accompany him until his short, stubby fingers would hardly obey him any longer. He had an even worse time at our house parties — only 'Frankfurter' dances in those modest days — at which, however, there was never any lack of charming women and girls. On these occasions our 'Bertl', as he was sometimes called ingratiatingly, had to play his latest waltzes over and over again, until the whole thing had turned itself into an endless Cotillion, so that the small, corpulent, little fellow, dripping with perspiration, was only able to regain his ease over the modest supper. No wonder that he deserted us occasionally and that, as a matter of fact, many a 'Schubertiad' had to take place without Schubert, if he did not happen to be in a social mood or if some guest or other was not particularly congenial to him. It was not uncommon for him to keep a company of invited guests waiting vainly for him, while he sat in comfort with half a dozen assistant schoolmasters, former colleagues of his, drinking wine in a secluded tavern. If we reproached him the next day, he would say with a contented chuckle: 'I was not in the mood!'

In 1825. Bauernfeld was twenty three, Schwind twenty one, and Schubert twenty eight; Bauernfeld records in his dairy in April that year:

I am still in love with Clotilde [his mistress] as Moritz is with Nettel [his very proper Catholic future fiancée]. Schubert sniggers at us both, but is not quite heart-whole himself.

The round of social activity was wearing Schubert down; there is also some evidence that he was beginning to find his constant companions irritating and immature despite their charm and liveliness. Vogl invited him to spend the summer in Steyr, and he left Vienna thankfully in May; his remark that happiness softens the mind and makes it frivolous had been (in his case) uncomfortably true that winter.

Schubert spent the whole summer of 1825 away from Vienna, mostly in Vogl's company. They did not remain all the time in Steyr, but paid extended visits to Linz, Gmunden, Salzburg and

Gmunden in the mid-
1820's (*from a lithograph
by Jacob Alt*)

Bad Gastein. For most of his long happy holiday Schubert travelled
as Vogl's guest, at his expense. Throughout the summer, wherever
they went, they gave recitals and there are many delighted reactions
in contemporary letters and diaries; everyone felt it was '. . . a
divine pleasure to hear these two'.

To Schubert's annoyance and sadness he did not see his beloved
friend Josef von Spaun when he was at Linz; Spaun happened to be
posted to another town. Schubert wrote to him:

Linz without you is like a body without a soul, like a headless horseman, or
like soup without salt . . .

But at least Schubert was staying with great friends of Spaun's, the
Ottenwalt family, and there are valuable letters from Anton
Ottenwalt to Spaun proudly describing their brilliant guest, letters
which amongst other things make the first mention of the so-called
'Lost' Gmunden-Gastein symphony. Ottenwalt wrote to Spaun
in July:

By the way, he had worked at a symphony at Gmunden, which is to be
performed in Vienna this winter.

He also wrote a moving letter on 27 July describing the serious side
of Schubert's being, his depth and intellectual passion.

Schubert was so friendly and communicative, not only with Max [von Spaun, Josef's brother], which goes without saying, but with us too. On Sunday, after Vogl had left at 9.30, he remained with us: there were Max and I, Marie and Mama, who retired between 10 and 11 o'clock. We sat together until not far from midnight, and I have never seen him like this, nor heard: serious, profound and as though inspired. How he talked of art, of poetry, of his youth, of friends and other people who matter, of the relationship of ideals to life, &c.! I was more and more amazed at such a mind, of which it has been said that its artistic achievement is so unconscious, hardly revealed to and understood by himself, and so on. Yet how simple was all this! — I cannot tell you of the extent and the unity of his convictions — but there were glimpses of a world-view that is not merely acquired; and the share which worthy friends may have in it by no means detracts from the individuality shown by all this . . .

There are more letters from Schubert than usual that summer. A very long one to his father and stepmother begins rather stiffly but becomes relaxed and spirited. Having described his summer itinerary, and the weather — 'I grew positively thin from sheer perspiration' — he sends teasing messages to his brothers:

Kindest remembrances to Ferdinand and his wife and children. I suppose he still crawls to the 'Cross' and cannot do without Dornbach [both places where Ferdinand went to drink wine]; also, he has doubtless been ill 77 times again, and has thought 9 times that he was going to die, as though dying were the worst that can happen to a man! If only he could once see these heavenly mountains and lakes, the sight of which threatens to crush or engulf us, he would not be so attached to puny human life, nor regard it as otherwise than good fortune to be conscious of earth's indescribable power of creating new life. What is Karl doing? Is he going to travel or not? He must be busy now, for a married artist's duty is to supply works of nature as well as art, and if he succeeds in both kinds, he will be very praiseworthy, for that is no small matter. I renounce it myself . . . And now I must end this chatter at last, though I felt that I must substitute a long letter for a long silence. Marie, Pepi and little Probstl Andre I kiss 1,000 times. Besides, please remember me most kindly to all who are mindful of me. In expectation of a speedy reply, I remain, with all my love,

Your
most faithful son
Franz.

The Lueg Pass near
Gastein

It is to his stepsisters and stepbrother he sends 1,000 kisses; this is the warmest of his surviving letters to his parents. He is definite to his father about renouncing the idea of marriage and family; whether he fully realized the dangers of syphilis, that not only was it infectious but was passed on to offspring, we do not know;

109

perhaps it was simply the thought of his three brothers Ferdinand, Karl and Ignaz all tied down to domesticity which made him state so firmly in this letter that such a life was not for him. Yet he was fond of children he knew and with his easy good humour appealed very much to them.

While in Gmunden, Schubert and Vogl stayed with the Traweger family who had a house near a landing stage right on the Traun lake. The five-year-old son, Edward Traweger, became very attached to Schubert, and later in life described that holiday.

Hardly was I awake in the morning when, still in in my nightshirt, I used to rush in to Schubert. I no longer paid morning visits to Vogl because once or twice, when I disturbed him in his sleep, he had chased me out as a 'bad boy'. Schubert in his dressing-gown, with his long pipe, used to take me on his knee, puffed smoke at me, put his spectacles on me, rubbed his beard against me and let me rumple up his curly hair and was so kind that even we children could not be without him . . . The men were always very pleasant and gay; they made excursions and went sailing and my good father, who had a great talent for entertaining and knew just how to organize things, was blissfully happy. He always spoke of Schubert with enthusiasm and was attached to him with all his heart.

During August and September he wrote eight fine songs, amongst them *Delphine* one of his least-known masterpieces. *Delphine* was composed at Steyr, where Schubert and Vogl were spending a final two weeks at the end of September. It is a woman's song, and shows Schubert's deep understanding of the female psyche. The whole song is a passionate outpouring of a woman in love, whose love is reciprocated, yet:

> *How can joy give me so much pain?*

The pain inherent even in a happy love affair, the obsessive fervour and utter dependence of this woman's love is beautifully suggested by Schubert's setting of the words:

> *Now that I love, I begin to wish to live,*
> *   and I die.*
> *Now that I love, I wish to burn brightly,*
> *   and I fade.*

Delphine is one of the finest women's love songs ever written, and ranks with the best of Schubert. It is an excellent example of his treatment of the strophic song; there are in *Delphine* basically four verses, with a repeated refrain, but the arrangement is so rich for both voice and piano that it has the seamlessness of a *durch-componiert* song. It is a long and very difficult song, but a great interpreter of it, Janet Baker, says of her own approach:

Bad Gastein, 1800 (*from an aquatint by Johann Jacob Strütt*)

Speaking generally, I found some years ago that my own personal 'key' to Schubert lay in an approach of absolute simplicity. One is inclined to come to the songs with awe — rightly so of course, but if one scrupulously obeys the written marks on the score with a mind uncluttered, childlike almost, the songs work. After that, the performer 'grows' into each Lied and gradually perceives the different levels of significance which long association brings.

It is interesting to see how closely her views about performance coincide with Leopold Sonnleithner's of a hundred years before. Schubert's songs speak for themselves; they do not need to be 'acted', however dramatic their tone. But they are robust too, and however rough and insensitive a singer's onslaught, some of the magic always remains.

111

Chapter 9

Poverty and Struggle

'A tune was for Schubert the most natural way of releasing emotion.' —
J. A. Westrup

A large and varied amount of Schubert's music was published during 1825; no less than four publishers issued his work, and yet it failed mysteriously to catch the attention of Vienna, and thereby of musical Europe. It is an excellent selection of Schubert at his best, his most serious and significant: Diabelli published three Goethe songs; Cappi brought out several more songs, dances and a piano duet; Sauer and Leidesdorf published the Piano Duet in A flat and six *Grandes Marches* dedicated to Schubert's doctor, Bernhardt; while Pennauer brought out the lovely Sonata in A major (which Schubert had been playing during the summer to delighted listeners) and finally three songs, including *Die Junge Nonne*. The last two publishers were not well-known, but their distribution appears to have been adequate. The newspapers reviewed the works more or less favourably; yet even these publications did not make the Viennese see Schubert as a major composer.

One of the reasons certainly lay in the fact that Schubert was in no sense a public performer. He had a pleasant high baritone voice but was no soloist. He played the piano with delicacy and precision, but he was not a virtuoso pianist like Mozart or Beethoven. (This also may be the reason why Schubert, with all his love of the piano, never wrote or even considered writing a piano concerto.) His string playing was confined to his private musical life; he did not conquer the public by that certain method, a successful popular opera. He was not interested in pandering to public taste.

Thus for the Viennese he was merely an obscure song-and-dance writer whose songs tended to be on the difficult side, but whose dances were delightful. Perhaps his music in general lacked some quality his contemporaries of Biedermeier Vienna looked for. M. J. E. Brown makes a perceptive assessment:

The very elements which many music lovers find most congenial are either absent altogether in his music, or only briefly encountered: wit, understatement, sophistication, picturesqueness, delicacy, bravura. These attractive qualities must be sought elsewhere, in the songs and piano pieces and orchestral suites of other men. Schubert's song-texts are neither erotic nor cynical. His expression is full-blooded, personal, extravagant, and the nearest he gets to humour, as Richard Capell has said, is good-humour; but it is not an urbane expression, nor an introverted one, and it is the power already spoken of, by which his music achieves sublimity, and radiates a 'light that never was on sea or land', that raises him above the level of the lesser composers, who are otherwise almost his equals in melodic charm and the affectionate spirit.

This power is the last thing contemporaries are aware of; it is the prime quality revealed only by the passage of time.

A final cause of Schubert's lack of renown in his own city was possibly his unprepossessing exterior.

Schwind, asked by a Viennese lady what Schubert looked like, answered in his devastating way: 'Like a drunken cabby!'

Schubert looked in no way the composer of people's imagination; a contemporary admirer, Louis Schlösser, describes how he expected the creator of such beauty to have

Franz Lachner, Franz Schubert and Eduard von Bauernfeld in Grinzing. Pencil sketch by Schwind

the advantage of physical beauty as well! Great was my disappointment when Schubert, whose personality interested me so extraordinarily, appeared on the platform and I saw, in this rather awkward, almost clumsy figure, in the strongly domed head, in the gentle, though anything but spirited features, the tone poet whom my dreams had identified with the grace and forms of the youthful Antinous . . .

Those who did not know Schubert personally were put off by his manner as well as his looks. An embassy official, Frank von Andlau, found that:

his personality was of the most disagreeable kind. He shared with Beethoven his shy withdrawal from the world, his gloomy bearing; one would never have suspected in this wooden appearance, in this unprepossessing exterior, the greatly gifted creator of so many wonderful songs.

Luckily his friends have left us vivid descriptions of what Schubert was really like in his maturity, both in public and in private. Leopold Sonnleithner, for instance, gives a full and most detailed description:

Schubert was below average height, with a round, fat face, short neck, a not very high forehead, and thick, brown, naturally curly hair; back and shoulders rounded, arms and hands fleshy, short fingers, *main potelée*; his

eyes (if I am not mistaken) grey-blue, eyebrows bushy, nose stubby and broad, lips thick; the face somewhat negroid. The colour of his skin was fair rather than dark, but it was inclined to break out into little pimples and was somewhat darker because of this. His head sat somewhat squeezed between his shoulders, inclining rather forward — Schubert always wore spectacles. In repose, his expression appeared dull rather than vivacious; sullen rather than cheerful; one could have taken him for an Austrian, or more likely for a *Bavarian*, peasant. Only if one observed him more closely did his features become slightly animated when there was interesting music or entertaining conversation; the corners of his mouth turned up, his eyes sparkled and his whole bearing grew rather tense. He was only really animated among intimate friends, when there was wine or beer; but even then he never laughed freely and openly, but only managed a chuckle which sounded toneless rather than bright. Shy and taciturn, especially in smart society, which he only frequented in order to accompany his songs, more or less as a favour. Whilst doing this his face wore the most serious expression, and as soon as it was over he withdrew into a neighbouring

114

room. Indifferent to praise and applause, he shunned compliments and was content if his intimate friends gave him evidence of their satisfaction.

Josef von Spaun is as usual careful to right wrong impressions; Victorian pictures of Schubert, he says angrily, make him look 'ugly and Negroid':

but anyone who knew him will be forced to contradict that. The portrait of Schubert painted by Rieder, and engraved, is extraordinarily like him. Looking at it, one can judge for oneself whether the face is ugly and negroid. Just as little can one say that Schubert was handsome; but he was well formed and when he spoke pleasantly, or smiled, his features were full of charm, and when he was working, full of enthusiasm and burning with zeal, his features appeared sublimated and almost beautiful.

So far as his body is concerned, one might imagine him as a fat lump, from the descriptions in the biography. But that is entirely incorrect. Schubert had a solidly built, thick-set body but there was no question of his being fat or having a paunch. His very youthful friend, Moritz Schwind, exceeded him in girth even in those days.

Finally, Anselm Hüttenbrenner's description of Schubert adds a few new details:

Schubert's outward appearance was anything but striking or prepossessing. He was short of stature, with a full, round face and was rather stout. His forehead was very beautifully domed. Because of his short sight he always wore spectacles, which he did not take off even during sleep. Dress was a thing in which he took no interest whatever; consequently he disliked going into smart society, for which he had to take more trouble with his clothes. As a result many a party anxiously awaited his appearance and would have been only too glad to overlook any negligence in his dress; sometimes, however, he simply could not bring himself to change his everyday coat for a black frock coat; he disliked bowing and scraping, and listening to flattering talk about himself he found downright nauseating.

Schubert in 1827 (*oil painting by W. J. Mähler*)

Hüttenbrenner's remark that Schubert slept in his spectacles is echoed by many of his friends, Bauernfeld, however, says he found Schubert 'still in bed, fast asleep, with his spectacles on his head as usual'; *on* his head — as if they were pushed up, which indeed would have been more comfortable, but is eccentric nonetheless.

So for many Schubert 'was to outward appearances a lump of dough', yet 'his eyes had such a sparkle that the inner fire was revealed at the first glance'. His character was attractive; people of many different types were usually drawn to him. He was obviously great fun to be with; the 'drunken cabby' was the most delightful company for those whom he loved.

While Schubert was on holiday with Vogl both Schober and Kupelwieser returned to Vienna.

To Schober and Kupelwieser I look forward with curiosity, to the former as to a man whose plans have miscarried, and to the latter as wearing the look of one coming from Rome and Naples.

Anna Hönig (*drawing in Indian ink by Schwind*)

wrote Schubert to Bauernfeld, in reply to a letter asking him to share rooms with Schwind and Bauernfeld. Schubert agreed to the idea in principle, but was cautious 'about such bachelors' and students' plans', particularly, he says, since Schwind's recent letters have been full of nonsensical brainless chatter. Despite this slight detachment, when Schubert finally arrived back in Vienna and was reunited with his friends, he spent his entire time in their company and did no composing until December. Bauernfeld wrote in his diary in October:

Schubert is back. Inn and coffee house gathering with friends, often until two and three in the morning.

> Shamefully, we confess
> Every night
> Drinking and laziness
> Give us delight.

Schober is the worst in this. True, he has nothing to do, and actually does nothing, for which he is often reproached by Moritz.

Bauernfeld's diary becomes a useful source of information on Schubert's circle from this point onwards. He wrote an interesting analysis of the young men in March 1826:

Schober surpasses us all in mind, and much more so in speech! Yet there is much in him that is artificial, and his best powers threaten to be suffocated in idleness — Schwind's is a glorious, pure nature — though always fermenting, as if he were going to burn himself out. — Schubert has the right mixture of the idealist and the realist. The world seems fair to him. — Mayrhofer is simple and natural, for all that Schober asserts that he is a kind of easy-going intriguer. — And I? Ah, if one could know oneself! Until I have done something worth while I am no human being.

Looked at as a whole, that winter was a bad patch for Schubert; he was short of money and often without his usual consuming urge to work. January was a good month, in which he composed four songs from Goethe's *Wilhelm Meister*, and four other songs including a partsong to words by Schober, but there is nothing recorded in February. A burst of songs and waltzes in the spring coincided with his application for the vacant post of Musical Director to the Court Chapel. He very much needed a job of some sort, but he did not get this one. Another attempt to write an opera was planned, to a libretto by Bauernfeld, who did not begin it until May, when on an extended holiday tour with Mayrhofer. His description of the story is enough to show us that poor Schubert would be presented with another turgid and romantic melodrama:

. . . I thought of the libretto for Schubert and set to work on *Der Graf von Greichen*. Dramatic and musical contrasts; orient and occident; janissaries and knighthood, romantic wooing and wedded love etc. — in short, a Turkish-Christian outline.

Schubert, stuck in Vienna, complains to Bauernfeld of its boredom and emptiness and ends his letter:

I am not working at all. — The weather here is truly appalling, the Almighty seems to have forsaken us altogether, for the sun simply refuses to shine. It is May, and we cannot sit in any garden yet. Awful! appalling!! ghastly!!! and the most cruel thing on earth for me. Schwind and I intend going to Linz with Spaun in June . . .

But this plan came to nothing; Schubert wrote again to Bauernfeld in July:

I cannot possibly get to Gmunden or anywhere else, for I have no money at all, and altogether things go very badly with me. I do not trouble about it, and am cheerful.

For the rest, come to Vienna as soon as possible. As Duport [Barbaja's authorized representative at the Kärntnertor Theatre] wants an opera from me, but the libretti I have so far set do not please at all, it would be splendid if your libretto were favourably received. Then at least there would be money, if not reputation as well!

Schwind is quite in the dumps about Nettel! Schober is a privileged business man. *Vogl is married*!!

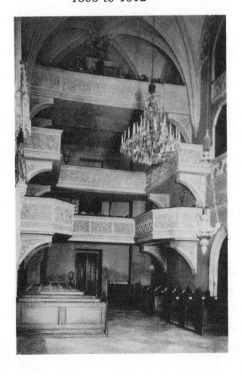

The Hofkapelle (Court Chapel) in the Imperial Palace, where Schubert sang in the choir from 1808 to 1812

Schwind's fiancée Anna (Nettel) Hönig had criticised him for his lack of religion, and goaded by this he had said to her: 'Go and fall in love with the Pope!', a remark which did not endear him. Michael Vogl's marriage to Kunigunde Rosa had not only amazed Schubert, but also effectively removed from his life one of his financial props, for it had been Vogl who had paid for some of his holidays in the past, and this would no longer happen. Vogl no longer needed the composer's companionship.

But the July letter to Bauernfeld is basically cheerful in tone because Schubert had started composing again with all his old fiery vigour. Between the 20th and 30th of June he wrote his greatest and last string Quartet, in G major. This work is full of inspired innovations, such as the use of a 'double-theme', instead of the more usual double representation of the one main theme which occurs in his earlier chamber works. This weaving together of two main themes is a fine device which Schubert used again in his last great instrumental works, particularly in the String Quintet in C and the last symphony.

In the last Quartet Schubert wrote music 'of the grandest, noblest order' (Brown), but also music intensely 'modern' and difficult; he introduced unexpected and harsh harmonic changes and often discarded classical tonality entirely; he made no attempt to please contemporary listeners. Indeed, they found his music very hard to take; his effects were so new and revolutionary that few could understand what he was doing. To illustrate the puzzlement people felt, there is a fascinating letter written by the composer Schumann in November 1829 describing a duet of Schubert's he played:

I remember playing that very Rondo at an evening party at Herr Probst's, but at the finish both players and listeners stared at one another, rather at a loss to know what to think, or to know what Schubert meant by it all . . .

But it was not difficult string quartets that everyone wanted from him, it was an opera. There was a particularly gifted new soprano, Nanette Schechner, singing in Vienna, whom Schubert admired. Schober (no longer quite the intimate soul-mate of Schubert's that he had been) wrote petulantly to Bauernfeld that summer:

If only Schubert would write an opera for her, perhaps yours would be suitable. If only he were not such a naïve barbarian. When I asked him recently why he had not come to see me during the whole of my illness, he answered innocently: 'But you are never at home' — . . . Today Schubert is to come out here; I hope he will keep his word.
[Schober was at Währing for the summer.]

At the end of July Bauernfeld returned to Vienna; he describes it in his diary:

When we landed at Nussdorf [near Währing] in the evening, Schwind and Schubert ran to meet me out of the coffee-house. Great rejoicing! — 'Where is the opera?' — Asked Schubert. 'Here!' — I solemnly handed him 'The Count of Gleichen'. — To Schober at Währing. According to the old custom, we all spent the night together, and how much we had to tell!

The libretto never really inspired Schubert, though he worked on it spasmodically until his death. It was in fact prohibited by the censorship, but Schubert disregarded this. It is a great pity he wasted any time on it at all, when his other music was showing the development and stature found in the G major Quartet.

In August, penniless and ill, Schubert wrote letters to two music publishers in Germany, to Probst, and to Breitkopf and Härtel; of the two replies, only Probst was encouraging although all he

As each song was written, Schubert took it to Sophie Müller, a well-known singer and actress, for her opinion

118

'Promenade at the City Gate' by Moritz von Schwind, 1827. In many ways this picture anticipates Schwind's decision to leave the city of Vienna. He can be seen in the foreground studying a map, while his fiancée Anna Hönig looks on rather anxiously from over the garden wall. Among the promenaders are Schubert, Vogl and Bauernfeld

wanted was a few songs and piano compositions as long as they were 'agreeable and easily comprehensible'. Schubert sent him three works.

In Vienna itself, there were frequent and well-attended Schubertiads, and with the return of Vogl and his new wife in September, more recitals took place. Vogl's voice was going now, and he employed histrionic gestures to hide the fact. Spaun says Vogl 'overstepped the permissible limits more and more as he lost his voice, but nevertheless he always sang *strictly in time*; he merely helped himself out as well as he could, in the manner of the experienced opera singer, where his voice and strength did not suffice.' Schubert insisted on a strict timing and forgave Vogl many of his incidental eccentricities because of his excellent musicianship. He and Vogl resumed their friendship and together began visiting salons like Sophie Müller's again.

During the early autumn of 1826 Schubert was staying with Schober and his mother in a house very near the Seminary. Spaun, who was now living in Vienna, called on him there one morning in October while he was composing the G major sonata. Spaun describes the incident:

I found him one morning writing at a sonata. Although disturbed, he at once played me the first passage which he had just completed, and when I liked it very much he said, 'If you like the sonata, it shall be yours; I want

119

to give you as much happiness as I possibly can', and soon he brought it, as it is engraved, and dedicated to me. It is Op. 78.

Spaun's taste in music was very different from Schober's; the latter liked only the lighter music, and was out of sympathy with many we would now consider Schubert's masterpieces; Spaun on the other hand seems always to have loved Schubert's more difficult and ambitious music.

Schubert did not stay long with the Schobers; in November he moved into lodgings on his own near the ancient fortified wall leading to the Inner City; to reach him his friends walked along the wall, or bastion, and complained of the 'most frightful mud'. During the last part of 1826 there were a series of big Schubertiads, at Spaun's and at other houses; a record has been kept of them in the diaries of the brothers Fritz and Franz von Hartmann, friends of Spaun's, who stayed in Vienna from late 1826 until the end of 1827. They mixed constantly with Schubert's circle, and give us a clear picture of the social pattern, though one longs for greater fullness in their frequent mentions of Schubert.

The most vivid of all the memoirs of Schubert at this period are by Bauernfeld, whose dramatist's eye picked up detail and idiosyncrasy with telling effect. Despite the fact that these memoirs were written in 1869, it is worth quoting from them extensively, because in their liveliness they give us a picture of Schubert which feels right in essence, even if time has tempted Bauernfeld to elaborate. Here is a story showing a most vivid and unexpected side to Schubert:

It was on a summer's afternoon and, with Franz Lachner and others, we had strolled over to Grinzing for the 'Heuriger' [new wine], to which Schubert was especially partial, though I was quite unable to acquire a taste for its acute tartness. We sat over our wine, indulging in lively conversation, and it was not until the dusk of the evening that we walked back; I wanted to go straight home, as I was living in an outlying suburb at that time, but Schubert dragged me forcibly to an inn and I was not even spared the coffee-house afterwards, at which he was in the habit of winding up the evening, or rather the late hours of the night. It was already one o'clock and an extremely lively musical discussion had arisen over the hot punch. Schubert emptied glass after glass and had reached a sort of elated state in which, more eloquent than usual, he was expounding to Lachner and me all his plans for the future. At this point a singular misfortune had to bring a couple of professional artists, celebrated members of the Opera House orchestra, into the coffee-house. As these people came in Schubert stopped short in the middle of his impassioned discourse; his brow puckered, his small grey eyes gleamed out fiercely from behind his spectacles, which he pushed restlessly to and fro. But scarcely had the musicians caught sight of the master when they rushed up to him, grasped

View towards the suburb of Wieden

Vienna as seen from the bastions, about 1800

Schubert at the piano, with friends

Schubert portrait by H. J. Wesseling

Interior of a Vienna coffeehouse

him by the hands, paid him a thousand compliments and almost smothered him with flattery. Finally it transpired that they were extremely anxious to have a new composition for their concert, with solo passages for their particular instruments, and they were sure that *Meister* Schubert would prove accommodating, etc.

But the master turned out to be anything but accommodating; he remained silent. After repeated entreaties he said suddenly: 'No! For you I will write nothing.'

'Nothing for us?' asked the men, taken aback.

'No! Not on any account.'

'And why not, Herr Schubert?' came the rejoinder, in rather a nettled tone. 'I think we are just as much artists as you are! No better ones are to be found in the whole of Vienna.'

'Artists!' cried Schubert, hurriedly draining his last glass of punch and getting up from the table. Then the little man pulled his hat down over his ear and faced the *virtuosi*, one of whom was tall of stature, and the other more inclined to stoutness, as though threatening them. 'Artists?' he repeated. 'Musical hacks are what you are! Nothing else! One of you bites at the brass mouthpiece of his wooden stick and the other blows out his cheeks on the horn! Do you call that art? It's a trade, a knack that earns money, and nothing more! — You, artists! Don't you know what the great Lessing says? — How can anyone spend his whole life doing nothing but bite on a piece of wood with holes in it? — That's what he said — (turning to me) or something of the kind! Didn't he? (Once more to the *virtuosi*): You call yourselves artists? Blowers and fiddlers are what you are, the whole lot of you! I am an artist, I! I am Schubert, Franz Schubert, whom everybody knows and recognizes! Who has written great things and beautiful things, that you don't begin to understand! And who is going to write still more beautiful things — (to Lachner): that is so, my friend, isn't it? — the most beautiful things! Cantatas and quartets, operas and symphonies! Because I am not just a composer of *Ländler*, as the stupid newspapers say and as the stupid people repeat — I am Schubert! Franz Schubert! And don't you forget it! And if the word art is mentioned, it is *me* they are talking about, not you worms and insects, who demand solos for yourselves that I shall never write for you — and I know very well why! You crawling, gnawing worms that ought to be crushed under my foot — the foot of the man who is reaching to the stars — *Sublimi feriam sidera vertice* (to me): translate that for them! — To the stars I say, while you poor, puffing worms wriggle in the dust and with the dust are scattered like dust and rot!!'

A tirade like this, probably much worse but substantially just as I have given it, was flung at the heads of the dumbfounded *virtuosi*, who stood there gaping, unable to find a word in reply, while Lachner and I endeavoured to get the over-wrought composer away from the scene of the incident which, to say the least, was unpleasant. With soothing words we brought him home.

The next morning I hurried round to my friend's to see how things were, as his condition had seemed to me serious. I found Schubert still in bed, fast asleep, with his spectacles on his head as usual.

121

In the room his clothes of the previous day lay strewn about in wild disorder. On the writing-table lay a half-written sheet of paper, with a sea of ink spilled over it from the overturned ink-well. On the paper was written, '2 o'clock at night' — ... there followed a few half confused aphorisms, violent outbursts of feeling. There was no doubt he had written them down yesterday, after the violent scene... I waited for my friend to wake up. — 'So it's you?' he said, after he had recognized me, then he adjusted his spectacles and with a friendly smile, though almost embarrassed, offered me his hand. — 'Had your sleep out?' I asked with a certain emphasis. — 'What nonsense!' Schubert blurted out and, with a loud laugh, jumped out of bed. I could not refrain from mentioning the scene. 'What will people think of you?' I said, in a rather schoolmasterish tone of voice.

'The rogues!' replied Schubert quietly and good-naturedly. 'Don't you know they are the most scheming rascals in the world? At my expense too. They deserved the lesson! Though I am sorry about it. But I will write them the solos they asked for and they will still fawn on me for them. I know these people!'

There you have a bit of Schubert.

Bauernfeld says this was a remarkable episode, for Schubert was usually

amiable and modest, devoted to his friends from the bottom of his heart, and acknowledging with affection the achievements of others, as was shown, for example, by his ever recurring delight over each little drawing done by our highly gifted Schwind. For what was evil and false, on the other hand, he had a veritable hatred.

Bauernfeld describes Schubert's Austrian element 'uncouth and sensual' (Anton Ottenwalt called it his 'eagerly burning sensuality') and goes on:

If there were times, both in his social relationships and in art, when the Austrian character appeared all too violently in the vigorous and pleasure-loving Schubert, there were also times when a black-winged demon of sorrow and melancholy forced its way into his vicinity not altogether an evil spirit, it is true, since, in the dark consecrated hours, it often brought out songs of the most agonizing beauty. But the conflict between unrestrained enjoyment of living and the restless activity of spiritual creation is always exhausting if no balance exists in the soul. Fortunately in our friend's case an idealized love was at work, mediating, reconciling, compensating, and Countess Karoline may be looked upon as his visible, beneficent muse, as the Leonore of this musical Tasso.

Whatever the truth of this last remark, Bauernfeld had no doubts of the Countess Karoline's importance to Schubert.

Idealized love may have played its part in Schubert's life, but marriage was not going to. All round him, his friends were marrying; after Vogl, Leopold Kupelwieser married Johanna Lutz in September 1826 — Schubert insisted on playing the piano throughout the dancing at their wedding. Josef von Spaun was to marry in April 1826 at the age of 40. Although Schubert himself had renounced marriage, there must have been times in his last two years or so when the bitterness that he had no option overwhelmed him. No wonder he set the song which ends with the words:

My heart seems dead;
within it, her image stands rigid and cold;
if ever my heart should thaw
her image will melt away.

Chapter 10

Winterreise

'No matter how great our admiration for Schubert may be, we [the performers of his Lieder] only realize later in life what it is that raises him so far above the level of other composers: Schubert is *authentic*.' — Dietrich Fischer-Dieskau

The Vienna coffeehouse was an essential part of the life of Schubert and his circle, and the diaries of Fritz and Franz Hartmann describe the daily meetings in them. At this period, in 1826-1827, the Green Anchor was their favourite haunt — it is still standing today. Vienna was full of coffeehouses and inns like the Red Crayfish, the Blue Hedgehog, The Gate of Heaven, the Red Cross, the Crown of Hungary, and these places supplied most of the social and business needs of Viennese men, particularly of bachelors like Schubert. A coffeehouse was the equivalent of the English London club in its heyday. A Viennese coffeehouse served, besides coffee, wine and food, and if one was a regular habitué a room could be permanently reserved. Schubert's circle sometimes had this arrangement.

Entry after entry in the Hartmann diaries describe evenings of music at private houses, followed by an hour or two spent in a coffeehouse until about midnight. Both Hartmanns describe a Twelfth Night party and Schubertiad at Spaun's house which is as representative as any of a typical evening. From Franz von Hartmann's diary, 12 January 1827:

To Spaun's, where there is a Schubertiad. The dear Witteczek couple and his mother-in-law are there already; tall Huber too. Then, one by one, came Gahy, Schober, Schubert, Enderes, Walcher (who however had to leave before the music began), Moritz Pflügl (who has been in Paris), Lachner, a certain Rieder, Perfetta; finally Vogl and his wife, Bauernfeld, Schwind, Gross. We had a splendid sonata for four hands, glorious variations and many magnificent songs, among them a brand-new one (sung by Richard Coeur-de-Lion in 'Ivanhoe'), and old ones including 'Night and Dreams' and the 'Erl King'. A specially beautiful one, 'Sunset Glow' [Die Abendröte] by Lippe was sung twice by Vogl, who happened to be in an exceptionally good mood. Then we had a delicious repast, and several toasts were drunk. Suddenly Spaun arrived and said we must drink to brotherhood, which much surprised and pleased me. Then we had tossing

Vienna street scene showing exteriors of coffeehouses

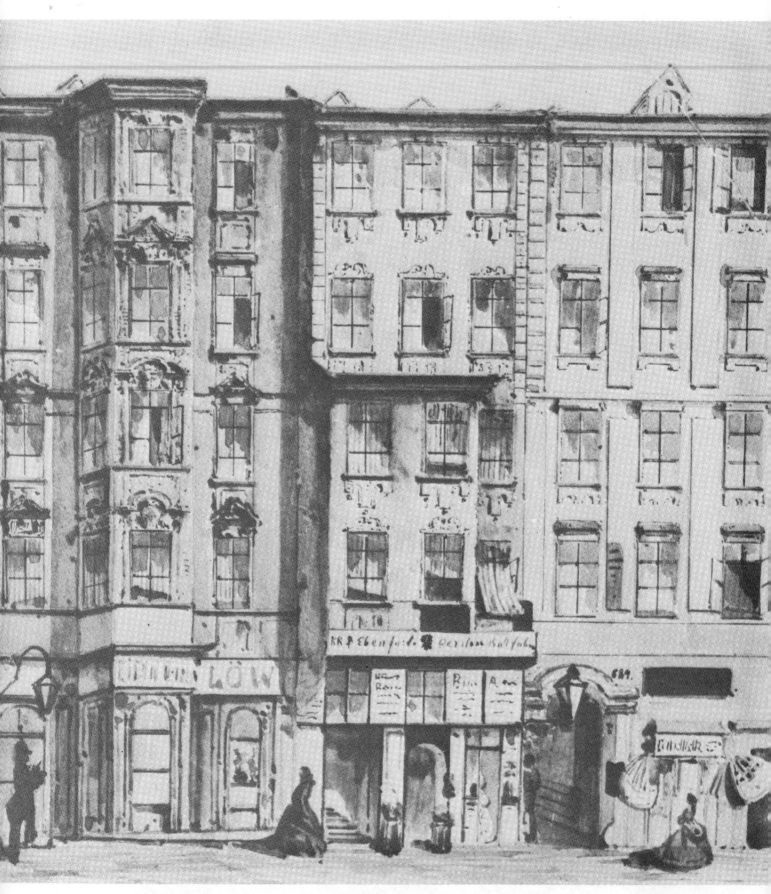

Artist's rendition of Bogner's Coffeehouse (See page 72.)

in a blanket (Enderes and Huber, the latter behaving very clumsily) and made the well-known beautiful star with four pairs. At last we took our leave of our kind hosts and went helter-skelter to Bogner's, where we smoked a few pipes, and in the street Schwind, running and flapping his cloak, gave a striking illusion of flying.

13th January 1827: We went to the "Anchor" where we found Spaun, Enderes, Gahy and Schober; Derffel too, at first. After having been there a long time and considering it time to adjourn, we went in glorious moonlight outside Bogner's cafe, where we danced and indulged in all kinds of childish performances.

The lighthearted gaiety of Schubert's life is also shown by a short note which was preserved amongst Schober's papers; the woman who wrote it in February 1827 to Schober and Schubert is not known.

We, by the grace of God ruler of all the halberdiers and janissaries, hereby take into arrest for the 15th inst., by virtue of this edict and in the name of a well-known, mathematically mapped-out power allied to Our-selves (*id est* Baroness Drossdick), the two well-nourished forms of a certain P. T. Schober and *ditto* Schubert. The aforesaid are to collaborate according to the powers of their minds and bodies in the glorification of a musical, declamatorical and dancical evening entertainment . . .

We exact implicit obedience on the part of our vassals.

Issued at our windy residence on St. Dorothea's Day.

Nina.

Yet against this background of good-natured fun and constant evening companionship Schubert lived his other life of intense composition. It was during this winter, 1827, that he began to write that compelling, often chilling, masterpiece, *Winterreise* (The Winter Journey). Spaun said, when discussing this song cycle:

Many people thought, and perhaps still think, that Schubert was a dull fellow with no feeling, but those who knew him better know how deeply his creations affected him and that they were conceived in suffering. Anyone who has seen him of a morning occupied with composition, aglow, with his eyes shining and even his speech changed, like a somnambulist, will never forget the impression. (And how could he have written these songs without being stirred to the depths by them!) In the afternoon he was admittedly another person, but he was gentle and deeply sensitive, only he did not like to show his feelings but preferred to keep them to himself.'

Spaun, knowing the intense level of creativity at which these songs were written, added:

There is no doubt in my mind that the state of excitement, in which he composed his most beautiful songs, and especially his *Winterreise*, contributed to his early death.

The Anchor Tavern

125

Schwind and Franz
Lachner passing
Schwind's picture of a
Turk on the entrance to
Bogner's Café — a sketch
by Schwind himself

Schubert and his friends did not fully understand the gravity of the disease festering inside him which weakened him yearly. Spaun's theory of the contributing cause of death is not really tenable, but there is no doubt that the sustained intellectual and creative effort involved in *Winterreise* would have exhausted Schubert, in his undermined state of health, more than was normal.

The poems of Wilhelm Müller had a specially powerful appeal for Schubert; when he came upon the first twelve poems of *Winterreise* in an almanack he was immediately inspired by them, and began to compose 'those incomparable scenes of despair and heartbreak, violence and numbness, in a landscape of snow and ice and bitter wind' (Brown). Late in the summer of 1827, Schubert came across Müller's complete version, which contained 24 songs in all, inserted between the twelve he had already set. Schubert promptly set these extra poems, but placed them in a group as the last half of his song cycle. This is a reason why the thread running through the poems is not so clear, and the construction not so taut, as in *Schöne Müllerin*. But *Winterreise* aims at a different effect; even in Müller's original sequence, the progress of his Winter Journey is not described dramatically but *hinted* at. The effect is impressionistic; story-line is no longer of importance, what matters is the emotional truth of the details, backwards and forwards in the journey, that both poet and composer fill out with such beauty and clarity.

The singer of these songs has been jilted by the girl he loves, whose constancy is like the weathervane on the roof of her house, swinging in the wind. Snow covers the earth, blotting out the green fields where she once walked arm in arm with him. There is the lime-tree on which he carved 'words of love'. Now he has to shut his eyes as he passes it, even though it is night.

> *The cold winds blew*
> *Straight into my face,*
> *my hat flew from my head —*
> *but I did not turn round.*

As he wanders, ice and snow reflect the pain in his heart; a frozen river hides a torrent beneath. His travelling is aimless; 'every path leads to the goal'; exhausted, he tries to find rest in a charcoal-burner's hut. His dreams, and the warmth of the images contrast starkly with his reality: flowers, green grass, hugs and kisses fill his brain

> *And when the cocks crowed*
> *my eyes opened;*
> *it was cold and dark*
> *and the ravens croaked from the roof-top.*

In his loneliness he finds a period of bright calm winter weather harder to bear than the storms. He hears a post-horn, and his heart leaps, pointlessly, because the post comes from his sweetheart's town.

Death enters his thoughts more clearly: he shudders at his own youth and black hair with no trace of grey:

how far off the grave still is!

He watches a carrion crow flying steadily above him and asks it:

Do you think my body will soon
fall prey to you?
Now, let me see — at last! —
constancy unto death.

He sees a last leaf on a tree and 'hangs' his hopes on it;

And should the leaf fall to the ground
My hope falls with it;
I too fall on the ground
and weep on the grave of my hope.

He hears dogs growling and barking in a sleeping village and cries for their barking to chase him away, since sleep is denied him; he welcomes a stormy morning, seeks hidden paths, finds himself in a graveyard, which he calls a 'cruel inn' because 'all the rooms in this

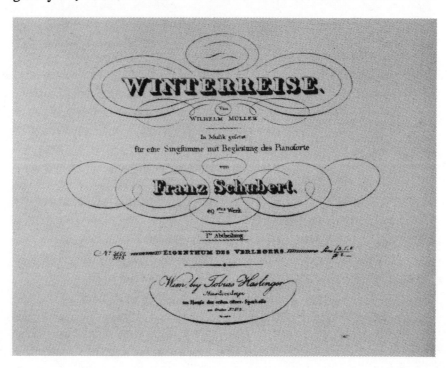

Title page of the first edition of *Winterreise* (Part 1), published in January 1828

house are already taken'. He turns away and presses on, a spirit of false hope and courage filling him:

> *Gaily on into the world,*
> *braving wind and weather!*
> *If there is no God on earth,*
> *we ourselves are gods!*

His sense of mental dislocation increases as he sees three suns in the sky — this phenomenon, scientifically described as a parhelion, becomes ominous and painful as the traveller says:

> *not long ago I had three suns —*
> *now the two best have gone down.*
> *If only the third would follow them —*
> *I shall feel better in the dark.*

This mood of hallucinated despair prepares one for the last song, *Der Leiermann* (The Hurdy-Gurdy Man), which I quote in full:

> *Over there, beyond the village, a hurdy-gurdy man stands,*
> *grinding away with numbed fingers as best he can.*
> *He staggers barefoot on the ice*
> *and his little plate remains ever empty.*
> *No one wants to hear him, no one looks at him*
> *and the dogs snarl about the old man.*
> *But he lets the world go by,*
> *he turns the handle, and his hurdy-gurdy is never still.*
> *Strange old man — shall I go with you?*
> *Will you grind your music to my songs?*

This poem was last in Müller's cycle too, and is a brilliant ending. The romantic simplicity of the earlier cycle with the straight-forward solution of death is left far behind; here instead there are complex implications of madness and living tragedy behind the haunting figure of the old man. It is too easy to say he is a symbol of death; he is in fact a more telling symbol: that of death-in-life.

This greatest of song cycles chilled Schubert's friends when they first heard it. Spaun describes the period of composition and first playing through:

For a time Schubert's mood became more gloomy and he seemed upset. When I asked him what was the matter he merely said to me 'well, you will soon hear it and understand'. One day he said to me 'Come to Schober's today, I will sing you a cycle of awe-inspiring songs. I am anxious to know what you will say about them. They have affected me more than any other songs.' So, in a voice wrought with emotion, he sang the whole of the

Franz von Hartmann
(*anonymous silhouette*)

'*Winterreise*' through to us. We were quite dumbfounded by the gloomy mood of these songs and Schober said he had only liked one song, '*Der Lindenbaum*'. To which Schubert only said, 'I like these songs more than all the others and you will get to like them too'; he was right, soon we were enthusiastic over the effect of these melancholy songs, which Vogl performed in a masterly way. More beautiful German songs probably do not exist and they were his real swan-song.

Schober, who liked a good lyrical tune, picked the one song where this occurs. The music of the rest of the cycle is stark, very advanced for its time; the treatment of thematic ideas is bold, new, and often demanding on the ear. No one could doubt Schubert's intellectual power after this. Once heard, no one could forget the magic way Schubert evokes the growling dogs in the sleeping village, or the posthorn, or the warm colours in the dreaming brain of the traveller, contrasted with the frozen harshness of his world.

In March 1827 Schubert moved into the Schobers' new lodgings in the Tuchlauben. He had the use of two rooms and a 'music closet': more space than he had ever had before. These lodgings became his base for the rest of his life. Clearly delighted with the unaccustomed spaciousness, he immediately invited all his friends round on 4 March to hear new compositions. But he then, typically, forgot all about it. Fritz von Hartmann was there:

Everyone was assembled, but friend Schubert did not come. At last Schwind undertook to sing several of Schubert's earlier songs which enchanted us. At half-past nine we all went to the 'Castle of Eisenstadt' [another favourite coffee-house] where Schubert arrived soon after us and won all hearts by his amiable simplicity, although he had deceived our hopes by his artist's negligence.

On 26 March, Beethoven died. The whole of Vienna mourned, and many, including Schubert and his circle, went to view the composer's body as it lay in state. Their attitude to death and to the dead body was very different from ours, as is clearly seen in Franz von Hartmann's vivid description of his visit.

28th March, 1827: Out to the Schwarzspanierhaus, where I contemplated the body of the divine Beethoven, who died the day before yesterday, at 6 in the evening. Already on entering his room, which is large and somewhat neglected, I was moved by its desolate look. It is scantily furnished, and only the pianoforte, of which the English made him a present, as well as a very fine coffin, struck a note of beauty in it. In some places lay music and several books. No catafalque had as yet been erected, but he still lay on the mattress of his bed. A cover was spread over him, and a venerable old man, whom I would regard rather as a servant than as a watcher, uncovered him for me. There I saw his splendid face, which unhappily I had never been able to see in life. Such a heavenly dignity lay spread over him,

Ludwig van Beethoven

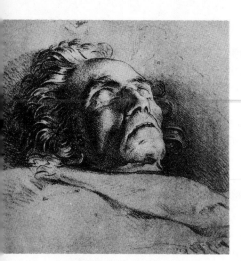

Beethoven on his deathbed (*lithograph by J. Danhauser*)

in spite of the disfigurement he is said to have suffered, that I could scarcely look my fill. I departed full of emotion; and only when I was downstairs could I have wept for not having begged the good old man to cut me off a few of his hairs. Ferdinand Sauter, whom I had arranged to meet, but whom I missed, ran across me, and I turned back with him, telling him of my plan. The old man showed him to us once more and also uncovered the chest for us, which, like the greatly swollen abdomen, was already quite blue. The smell of corruption was very strong already. We pressed a gratuity into the old man's hand and asked him for hair from Beethoven's head. He shook his head and motioned us to be silent. So we sadly trundled down the stairs, when suddenly the old man softly called us from the banisters upstairs, asking us to wait at the gate until the three fops had departed who were viewing the dead hero, tapping their swagger-canes on their pantaloons. We then re-ascended the stairs and, issuing from the door and putting his finger-tips to his lips, he gave us the hair in a piece of paper and vanished. We left, sorrowfully happy about it.

Their attitude was matter-of-fact, curious, respectful in its way but not sentimental or morbid; for Schubert and his world, death was death, and they had a robust interest in this ever-present phenomenon. Schubert wrote many songs about death, and has been accused of obsession with the subject; but if his attitude is compared with von Hartmann's, it falls into the correct perspective. Schubert was one of thirty-six torch bearers at Beethoven's funeral; they all wore 'funeral clothes with white roses and bunches of lilies tied to their arms with crêpe'.

During April that year there were several public performances of Schubert's music, including a successful first performance on Easter Monday of his Octet for Strings and Wind, written in 1824. There were several newspaper reviews; the Theatre Zeitung of 26 April said:

Herr Schubert's composition is commensurate with the author's acknowledged talent, luminous, agreeable and interesting; only it is possible that too great a claim may be made on the hearer's attention by its long duration. If the themes do not fail to recall familiar ideas by some distant resemblances, they are nevertheless worked out with individual originality. . .

Damning with faint praise; poor Schubert is not only longwinded but a plagiarist in their eyes. The form of this Octet was modelled on Beethoven's Septet in E flat, but there the resemblance ceases. As M. J. E. Brown says:

The octet gives us Schubert's everyday Vienna: his bohemianism, his sociability, his exuberance, his easy-going bonhomie; glimpses of the streets and fairgrounds of the city about him; a hint of the theatre, a snatch of

Johann Baptist Jenger
(*lithograph by Josef
Teltscher, 1826*)

song from the coffeehouse and beergarden; and all conveyed together with the sudden inspirational flash when the poetry and the picturesqueness of life in Vienna burn for a moment in his music.

Schubert managed to get away from Vienna twice during the spring and summer months. During May and June he went with Schober to Dornbach, a village outside Vienna. It was at Dornbach that Schubert composed *Das Lied im Grünen* (Spring Song) which is an exhilarating and joyful invocation of springtime. He also worked on sketches of *Der Graf von Gleichen*, Bauernfeld's opera libretto. Back in Vienna in July he composed his well-known part-song *Ständchen* (Serenade) to words by Grillparzer, which was performed as a surprise birthday present for a young girl, Louise Goșmar, in the garden of her house on a lovely summer's night.

Schubert's second holiday, in September, was in Graz, where he met up again with his old friend Anselm Hüttenbrenner. Schubert was travelling with Johann Jenger, and they stayed with Jenger's friend, the charming and accomplished Marie Pachler. The Pachlers were a very musical family and held frequent Schubertiads; Schubert's stay was relaxing in every way, and he wrote afterwards to his hostess that he had enjoyed 'the happiest days I have had for a long time'. While he was at Graz, he was clearly still working on Part II of *Winterreise*; he left a sketch of *Die Nebensonnen* (The False Suns) with the Pachlers. In October, back in Vienna, he made the final drafts and fair copies of these last twelve songs. (Part I of *Winterreise* was published in January 1828,

A view of the City Hall and Church from the Square in Graz

During his visit to Graz
Schubert stayed with
Madame Pachler

but Part II was not published until a month after Schubert's death; indeed, he is said to have corrected the proofs on his deathbed.)

1827 was a year in which Schubert concentrated on Lieder; he also wrote, besides his usual output of dances and other pieces for piano — Moments Musicaux and Impromptus — a Fantasia in C major for piano and violin, and his long and beautiful Trio in E flat, Opus 100, for piano, violin and cello. He composed this in November, and it received its first performance on Boxing Day, when it was played at a *Musikverein* concert with the gifted Schuppanzigh playing the violin. Its reception was enthusiastic, and this encouraged Schubert to make it the chief item in the concert of his own music he was to give the following March. The Trio is a leisurely and delightful piece of music, with an overall lightness but sureness of craftsmanship. The impressive piano part, when Schubert used the entire range of the Viennese piano, makes one wish he had turned his hand to a piano concerto.

The lightness and the entertaining dance-like rhythms in the finale of the Trio are in direct contrast to Schubert's own mood at the time: he was a sick man, with recurring headaches, giddiness and nausea, all those unpleasant symptoms of the second stage of his disease. He had to cancel engagements, and from a letter extant to Schwind's fiancée, Anna Hönig, it is clear that his physical condition depressed him in every way.

15 October

I find it very difficult to have to tell you that I cannot give myself the pleasure of being at your party this evening. I am ill, and in such a way which totally unfits me for such a gathering.

All his prospects were gloomy; apart from the ever present menace of his illness, his work on the opera was half-hearted despite his conviction that this was the only way he could gain proper recognition. A constant trickle of his works was being published, but they brought him little money and less fame.

For the average Viennese Schubert was a song-and-dance composer, a sort of Ivor Novello of his day; for the musical intelligentsia, his best work was becoming almost too 'modern', too avant-garde to understand. Thus he remained largely unappreciated. The strange icy, churning music of the last two songs of *Winterreise* would have alienated most contemporary listeners; Schubert's use of futuristic discords puzzled reviewers and public alike. Spaun summarized their attitude in his notes written in 1829 soon after Schubert's death:

His songs were gloomy, the accompaniment overladen, affected and too difficult, his transitions too daring, his pianoforte compositions turgid and

132

contrary to all the rules of keyboard writing, and for the theatre in particular he lacked any talent whatever; thus did a large part of public opinion express itself . . .

Spaun himself showed blind spots in his assessment of Schubert's music; there is a fascinating note, dated early 1829, to Bauernfeld in which he says:

In spite of all the admiration I have felt for my dear friend for years, I am of the opinion that in the field of instrumental and church music we shall never make a Mozart or a Haydn out of him, whereas in song he stands unsurpassed.

Spaun is in a sense to be forgiven in his view of Schubert's instrumental works: after all, when Schubert died the existence of the Unfinished Symphony was forgotten, and the two great instrumental works of 1828, the C Major Symphony and the String Quintet in C major, had never been performed. Thus Spaun's knowledge was incomplete; he based it only on those quartets he knew and the E flat Trio performed in December, and whatever works he had heard performed in Schubertiads.

Liechtental Church, where Schubert conducted his first Mass, in 1814

Spaun's comment about church music is, however, valid. As A. E. Dickinson says in his essay on 'The Choral Music',

Dispassionate analysis, unprejudiced by the compelling quality of the composer's best contemporary work, reveals in Schubert a foundation of voluble commonplace and of undistinguished melodic and structural formulae, inadequate for the text and inadequate for themselves.

It seems certain that Schubert found formal religion anything but 'religious': his songs imply he was a deeply religious man, yet except in a couple of letters of 1825 to his father and to his brother, he made no statement about his faith. In the letter to his father he described the effect on his audience of his song *Ave Maria*, a setting of a Walter Scott poem from 'The Lady of the Lake'.

They also wondered greatly at my piety, which I expressed in a hymn to the Holy Virgin, and which, it appears, grips every soul and turns it to devotion. I think this is due to the fact that I have never forced devotion in myself and never compose hymns or prayers of that kind unless it overcomes me unawares; but then it is usually the right and true devotion.

Schubert's letters to his father are stiff in tone, and we know that old Franz's sons found his rigid religious attitude excessive. This reference to the Virgin and to devotion was perhaps Schubert's effort to explain to his father that he was not godless. In a letter written to Ferdinand a month later, Schubert is moved to anger, while sightseeing, by the history of a massacre which was commemorated by a chapel; he exclaims:

Thou glorious Christ, to how many shameful actions must Thou lend Thy image: etc.

But apart from these two statements, we know little about Schubert's religious standpoint. There are the lines in *Winterreise* from *Mut* (Courage):

> *If there is no God on earth*
> *we ourselves are Gods,*

which Schubert's circle would have found more to their taste than any formal Christian credo. There is a revealing note to Schubert dated January 1827 from a coffeehouse friend of his, Ferdinand Walcher, which begins:

> *Cre-do in un-um De-um!*
> Not you, I know well enough . . .

Ferdinand Schubert
(*ivory relief by Norbert Schrödl, 1845*)

and as O. E. Deutsch points out, Schubert did omit the words *'Credo in unam sanctam catholicam et apostolicam ecclesiam'* from his Masses, but not the *'Credo'* proper. It is also interesting that in all the reminiscences written at the height of Victorian piety, Schubert's religious beliefs are not discussed. We can only conclude that he had discarded most of them; yet his music implies an intense inner spiritual life.

But his church music does not: he was never fired by the words of the liturgy as were Bach or Beethoven, who interpreted them afresh so that their meaning was heightened by the composer's own piety. Even Schubert's sixth and last Mass in E Flat, written just before his death, though his best, is nowhere in the same category of creative achievement as the masterpieces of that final great year.

135

Chapter 11

'The Singer is Called Away'

'Our portly, gay Schubert who considered himself less than the second best, indisputably and as a matter of course takes his place of honour among the foremost and greatest.' — Moritz von Schwind

At Schober's New Year's Eve party, after the clock struck twelve and the year 1828 began, Bauernfeld declaimed his specially written poem:

Roll onward, you ever revolving seasons
Into the abyss where we lose you for aye . . .

and so on for ten reverberating verses, bemoaning the passing of time:

Yet youth must at last to senility grow.

A verse about the fading of female beauty and then:

The spells of the poet, the pleasures of singing,
They too will be gone, be they true as they may;
No longer will songs in our party be ringing,
For the singer too will be called away.
The waters from source to the sea must throng,
The singer at last will be lost in his song.

The peculiarly prophetic quality of this verse is of course accidental; a poem or a play specially written for the occasion was simply part of the New Year's Eve pattern. Franz von Hartmann records the party:

1st January 1828: At Schober's. On the stroke of 12 we (Spaun, Enk, Schober, Schubert, Gahy, Eduard Rössler — a young medical student from Pest — Bauernfeld, Schwind and we two) drank together to a happy new year in Malaga. Bauernfeld then read a poem on that time of year. At 2 o'clock we went home . . .

A significant change was about to happen to Schubert's circle: Spaun became engaged that January to marry Franziska Roner; she was thirty, he now forty. When Spaun told Schubert, he replied:

While it makes me very sad that we are now going to lose you, you are right and have chosen well, and although I ought to be angry with your fiancée I should like to do something to please her. Invite her and I will bring Bocklet, Schuppanzigh and Linke and we will have some music as well.

Spaun goes on to say:

and that is what happened. Bocklet played a Trio with Schuppanzigh and Linke and afterwards, with Schubert, variations on an original theme for pianoforte duet, the latter with such fire that everyone was delighted and Bocklet embraced his friend with joy. We remained happily together until after midnight. It was the last evening of its kind.

As Kupelwieser had, so Spaun would now move away from his old bachelor routine; possibly with some relief, because in his heart Spaun never liked Schober, and there were always tensions between them which they kept under control simply because of their common affection for Schubert. As Spaun himself said: 'Through him we were all brothers and friends'.

The reading parties, discontinued some time before, were resumed that winter; Franz Hartmann records that the group read, amongst many things, Heinrich Heine's *Reisebilder* (Ideas on Travel) from which Schubert was to set the six great songs that are the last part of *Schwanengesang* (Swansong).

On 9 February, by a strange coincidence, two music publishers, Probst of Leipzig and Schott's Sons of Mainz, both wrote to Schubert asking to publish his work. Schott's letter was addressed simply to 'Franz Schubert, Esq Famous Composer in Vienna'. Schubert replied promptly to this letter:

Karl Maria von Bocklet
(*anonymous watercolour*)

Gentlemen,
I feel much honoured by your letter of 8th [sic] February and enter with pleasure into closer relations with so reputable an art establishment, which is so fit to give my works greater currency abroad.

I have the following compositions in stock:
a)   Trio for pianoforte, violin and violoncello, which has been produced here with much success.
b)   Two string Quartets (G major and D minor).
c)   Four Impromptus for pianoforte solo, which might be published separately or all four together.
d)   Fantasy for pianoforte duet, dedicated to Countess Karoline Esterházy.

e)   Fantasy for pianoforte and violin.
f)   Songs for one voice with pianoforte accompaniment, poems by
     Schiller, Goethe, Klopstock, et al., and Seidl, Schober, Leitner,
     Schulse, et al.
g)   Four-part choruses for male voices as well as for female voices with
     pianoforte accompaniment, two of them with a solo voice, poems by
     Grillparzer and Seidl.
h)   A five-part song for male voices, poem by Schober.
i)   'Battle Song' by Klopstock, double chorus for eight male voices.
k)   Comic Trio, 'The Wedding Roast' [*Der Hochzeitsbraten*], by
     Schober, for soprano, tenor and bass, which has been performed
     with success.

This is the list of my finished compositions, excepting three operas, a
Mass and a symphony. These last compositions I mention only in order to
make you acquainted with my strivings after the highest in art.

Now, if you should wish anything from the above list for publication, I
shall assign it to you with pleasure against a reasonable fee.

With all respect
Franz Schubert.

My address:
Under the Tuchlauben,
at the 'Blue Hedgehog,'
2nd floor.

The most interesting part of this touching and interesting letter is
the quick summary Schubert gives at the end of his less commercial
works; he mentions only three operas (he had finished eight in fact);
out of five Masses, he means only the A flat major; and which
symphony it is he singles out is not clear. Speculation over it leads
into the most complex aspect of the dating of Schubert's major
works: that of the last great symphony in C major, and its connec-
tion with the 'lost' symphony referred to earlier.

There are five references in 1824 and 1825 to a symphony, the
most specific being the remark of Anton Ottenwalt's quoted earlier,
when he wrote to Spaun in July 1825 with the remark that Schubert
'worked at a symphony in Gmunden, which is to be performed in
Vienna this winter'. This performance never took place. Some
scholars believe that this symphony, which they call the Gmunden-
Gastein, was lost, and there are many theories about how such a
catastrophe could happen.

The most likely and convincing theory is that Schubert sketched
out what was to be his great C major symphony that summer, and
put the draft manuscript aside for the time being, a habit we know
he had. M. J. E. Brown believed that Schubert returned to work on
it in February 1828 and completed the score in March, the date
Schubert put on the fair copy. (He often dated the fair copy, as he

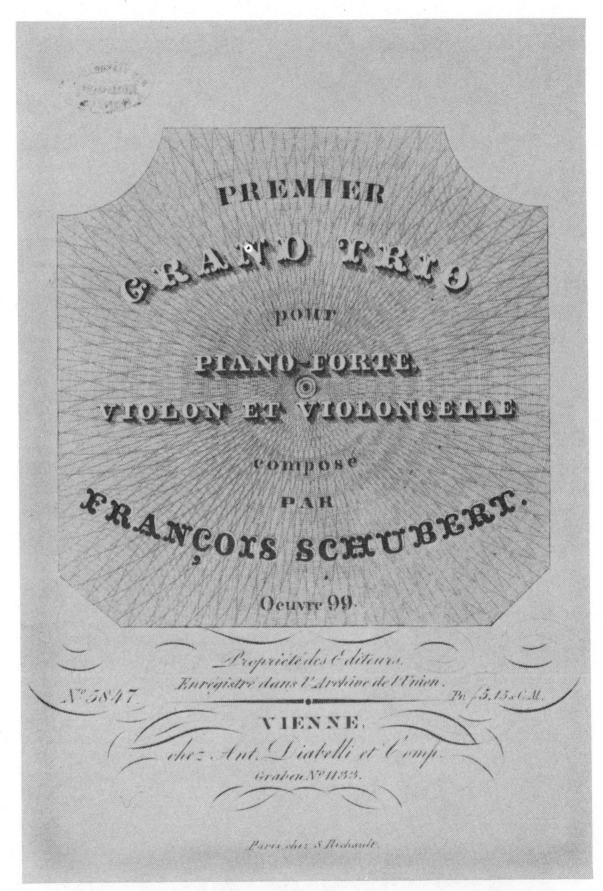

Title page of the first edition of the Piano Trio in B flat

Robert Schumann

Felix Mendelssohn

Franz Lachner's farewell concert in Vienna. Bauernfeld and Grillparzer are among those in the audience, with Schubert leading the applause (*drawing by Schwind*)

did part II of *Winterreise*, with no indication whatever of how long the work had been in progress.) This then is the symphony he mentions in his letter to Schott's Sons. Schubert sent the newly completed symphony to the Vienna *Gesellschaft der Musikfreunde*, to whom he had promised earlier to dedicate a symphony; they began to rehearse it, and found it too difficult to play. He then withdrew it, and substituted his earlier Symphony in C, written in 1818. His great C major Symphony then disappeared until the composer Schumann visited Ferdinand in 1839 and afterwards wrote excitedly to the publishers Brietkopf and Härtel: 'Some days ago I visited Franz Schubert's brother and I looked with astonishment at the treasures that are in his care'. As a direct result of this visit, Ferdinand sent the manuscript of the 9th Symphony to Felix Mendelssohn in Leipzig, where Mendelssohn himself conducted a cut version of it on 21 March 1839. Mendelssohn wrote to Ferdinand while returning the symphony:

There was great and sustained applause after each movement, and more important than that, all the musicians in the orchestra were moved and delighted by the splendid work . . . Thank you once more most cordially for the pleasure you have given us through this.

Schubert's ninth symphony is his orchestral masterpiece and for many the summit of his achievement in music. It is Schubert at his most dynamic and powerful, in a massive monumental work.

What he was now aiming at was the epic grandeur and classical objectivity of the Beethoven symphonies . . . Yet . . . though Schubert returns here to a more classical technique and way of thinking, he tries in vain to harness his vast sweeping ideas to the classical form. Hence the enormous dimensions, the colossal crescendos and terrific climactic explosions of this work. There is a kind of emotional dynamism behind it entirely different from Beethoven's intellectual fury. (Mosco Carner)

The symphony opens on a slow horn theme, familiar but always haunting, a theme which grows in power throughout the movement until at the end it is played gloriously loud and rich with a full orchestra. The second movement, the Andante, with its novel treatment of brass instruments as 'utterers of poetic ideas instead of mere reinforcers of noise', is quintessential Schubert; M. J. E. Brown sums up that it is

his poetry and passion, his tender response, his technical gifts of thematic development, his use of the orchestra . . . and, above all, that subjective intensely personal approach to the listener which woos and wins his affection.

The Scherzo with its ferocious violence and length prepares us for that momentous, volcanic finale, unique in all music with its headlong speed and rhythmic impetus; the extraordinary length of the movement (1154 bars) reinforces its colossal effect. The whole symphony is a triumphant fusion of classical form and romantic spirit.

* * *

For a long time Schubert's friends had urged him to organise a concert devoted to his own music. Bauernfeld told Schubert roundly:

Do you want my advice? Your name is on everybody's lips and each new song of yours is an event! You have also composed the most glorious string quartets and trios — not to mention the symphonies! Your friends are delighted with them, but for the moment, no art dealer wants to buy them and the public still has no idea of the beauty and charm which lie hidden in these works. So make an effort, conquer your laziness, give a concert next winter — just your own things, of course! Vogl will help you with pleasure; Bocklet, Böhm and Linke will consider it an honour to place their virtuosity at the service of a *Maestro* like you; the public will scramble for tickets, and even if you don't become a Croesus at one fell swoop, a single concert will still suffice to cover your expenses for the whole year. Such a concert can be repeated every year and if the novelties make a furore, as I have no doubt they will, you can force up your Diabellis, Artarias and Haslingers, with their niggardly fee, into the immeasurable! So give a concert! Take my advice! Give a concert!

'Perhaps you may be right', replied my friend thoughtfully, 'if only I did not have to ask the fellows!' [professional musicians]

He did ask them, however, and the concert took place in the spring of 1828. . .

First page of the last movement of the Symphony No. 9

Einladung

zu dem Privat Concerte, welches Franz Schubert am 26 März, Abends 7 Uhr im Locale des österreich. Musikvereins unter den Tuchlauben N.° 558 zugeben die Ehre haben wird.

Vorkommende Stücke

1. Erster Satz eines neuen Streich- Quartetts, vorgetragen von den Herren Böhm, Holz Weiß und Linke

2. a) Der Kreutzzug von Leitner
   b) Die Sterne von demselben
   c) Der Wanderer a. d. Mond v. Seidl
   d) Fragment aus dem Aeschylus
   } Gesänge mit Begleitung des Piano-Forte vorgetragen von Herrn Vogl k. k. pensionirten. Hofopernsänger

3. Ständchen von Grillparzer, Sopran Solo und Chor vorges. von Fräulein Josephine Fröhlich und den Schülerinnen des Conservatoriums

4. Neues Trio für das Piano Forte, Violin und Violoncelle, vorgetragen von den Herren Carl Maria von Boklet, Böhm und Linke

5. Auf dem Strome von Rellstab. Gesang mit Begleitung des Horn's und Piano-Forte. vorgetragen von den Herren Tietze. und Lewy dem Jüngern

6. Die Allmacht. von Ladislaus Pyrker, Gesang mit Begleitung des Piano Forte. vorgetragen von Herrn Vogl

7. Schlachtgesang von Klopstock, Doppelchor für Männerstimmen.

Sämtliche Musikstücke sind von der Composition des Concertgebers

Eintrittskarten zu f 3 W. W. sind in den Kunsthandlungen der Herren Haslinger, Diabelli und Leidesdorf zu haben.

Announcement of Schubert's first (only) public concert

The actual date was 26th March, in the concert hall of the *Gesellschaft der Musikfreunde* in the Tuchlauben, in the same street in which Schubert lived. This very concert was recreated in London on its 150th anniversary, in March 1978, and the choice of music and the order in which it was played was revealing, both of Schubert's intentions and of his musical world. He opened his concert with the first movement only of a 'new' quartet, believed to be the G major of 1826; then four songs, mostly of very recent composition, were performed by Vogl; then *Ständchen* (1827), the serenade for Soprano, solo and chorus, which was a substitute for the cantata *Mirjam's Siegesgesang* (Miriam's Song of Triumph), an ambitious Handelian work which Schubert did not manage to finish in time. The next work was the main item, the successful but long Trio for piano, violin and cello, Opus 100; then there were three more songs, all of considerable weight: *Auf dem Strom* (1828) (On the River) with its horn obbligato; *Die Allmacht* (1825) (Omnipotence), a lengthy song with piano accompaniment performed by Vogl; and the final song and last item, *Schlachtgesang* (Battle Song), a rousing double chorus for male voices.

It was obvious from his choice of the string quartet movement to start the concert off, that Schubert meant to show the audience an example of his most dense and advanced writing while its concentration was fresh. The Trio had already been tried successfully in public, but most of the songs were examples of his recent work which he hoped would impress and appeal.

'Enormous applause, good receipts,' wrote Bauernfeld after the concert. But if Schubert and his friends waited eagerly for notices in the Viennese papers, they were doomed to disappointment. Amazingly, considering the space already afforded to Schubert previously, not *one* Viennese paper reported the concert. Short notices in Leipzig, Dresden and Berlin papers tell us why: the virtuoso violinist Niccolo Paganini had just arrived in Vienna. The *Dresden Abendzeitung* reported:

There is but one voice within our [Vienna's] walls, and that cries: 'Hear Paganini!' . . . [at] a private concert given by the favourite composer Schubert . . . there was unquestionably much that was good among it all, but the minor stars paled before the radiance of this comet in the musical heavens . . .

The complete lack of proper notices must have been distressing, but there was a compensation: at the end of March a long and sensitive review of *Winterreise* was published in the *Theaterzeitung*. For the very first time a newspaper critic seems to have sensed the full measure of Schubert's genius and his place in contemporary German romanticism.

Schubert has understood his poet [Müller] with the kind of genius that is his own. His music is as naïve as the poet's expression; the emotions contained in the poems are as deeply reflected in his own feelings, and these are so brought out in sound that none can sing or hear them without being touched to the heart. Schubert's mind shows a bold sweep everywhere, whereby he carries every one away with him who approaches him, and he takes them through the immeasurable depth of the human heart into the far distance, where premonitions of the infinite dawn upon them longingly in a rosy radiance, but where at the same time the shuddering bliss of an inexpressible presentiment is companioned by the gentle pain of the constraining present which hems in the boundaries of human existence. Herein lies the nature of German romantic being and art, and in this sense Schubert is a German composer through and through, who does honour to our fatherland and our time. It is this spirit that is breathed by the present songs; it expresses itself through them even where the subject seems to point to entirely different paths; and in this logical establishing of

142

harmony between outward and inward things lies the chief merit of both poets, the speaking and the singing one.

Schubert's concert was a success, however, for those who heard it; 'Everybody was lost in a frenzy of admiration and rapture' wrote one admirer. And it made him some money; indeed what with these proceeds and the selling of his work to his two new publishers, Schott's Sons and Probst, Schubert was temporarily in funds. His friends benefited; there is an entry that spring in Bauernfeld's diary:

Heard Paganini! The admission [over twice the price of Schubert's own concert] was paid for me by Schubert.

(Ironically, Schubert was a great admirer of Paganini, and described his playing to Anselm Hüttenbrenner: 'I have heard an angel sing in the Adagio . . .')

The spring of 1828 was thus a time of creative and financial stability for Schubert. In fact, stability of one kind or another was overtaking his circle: Spaun got married in April, Leopold Sonnleithner married the Louise of Ständchen, Schwind became formally engaged to his long-time unofficial fiancée, Nettel Hönig; Bauernfeld was increasingly occupied by his official duties and his various literary activities.

Schubert's health remained poor, but it did not seem to curtail his life that spring and summer. His finances did not remain good for long, and lack of money caused him to spend the whole summer in Vienna despite plans to visit the Pachlers in Graz and the Trawegers in Gmunden. Johann Jenger, with whom he had gone to Graz before, wrote to Marie Pachler on 4 July, describing Schubert's 'not very brilliant financial circumstances . . . He is still

Gmunden

143

here at present, works diligently at a new Mass and only awaits still — wherever it may come from — the necessary money to take his flight into Upper Austria.' The necessary money never came.

The Mass mentioned by Jenger is Schubert's sixth, finished in July. During 1828 he had begun to compose church music again, after three years in which he wrote only one single work for the church, the so-called 'German Mass', popular and greatly loved by the Viennese to this day. (In fact it is not a Mass at all, but a series of eight separate religious songs by J. Neumann to be sung by choir and congregation between the various stages of the Office of Low Mass. It is an attractive but light-weight and slightly sentimental work.)

Yet in 1828, after more or less leaving liturgical composition behind him, Schubert began, despite his lack of sympathy with overt Christian practice, to write church music again. A complete list of compositions during the last year of his life reveals the varied pattern of his intense creative activity, again at a phenomenal level:

January
Commencement of Fantasia in F minor, Pianoforte Duet.
Der Tanz (The Dance), Schnitzer. For Soprano, Alto, Tenor and Bass, with pianoforte.
Der Winterabend (The Winter Evening) Leitner
Die Sterne (The Stars) Leitner
February and March
Symphony in C major, The 'Great' — begun probably in 1825, finished in March.
Mirjams Siegesgesang (Miriam's Song of Triumph), Grillparzer, Soprano solo and mixed chorus with pianoforte accompaniment.
Auf dem Strom (On the River), Rellstab
Lebensmut (or 1826?) (Life's Courage) Rellstab
April and May
Fantasia in F minor, finished (Bauernfeld called it a 'new, wonderful four-handed Fantasy')
Herbst (Autumn), Rellstab
Drei Klavierstücke Pianoforte solo.
Hymne an den Heiligen Geist, Schmidl, for male chorus Allegro in A minor — pianoforte duet
June and July
Fugue in E minor for pianoforte or organ duet (a trifling piece composed for a bet)
Mass No. 6 in E flat
Rondo in A major, pianoforte duet
Psalm XCII (Hebrew Text), soloists and mixed chorus
August
Glaube, Hoffnung, Liebe (Belief, Hope and Love) by Reil — soloists, chorus and wind band.

144

Schubert's brother Ignaz: oil painting by his stepson, Heinrich Hollpein

Glaube, Hoffnung und Liebe, Kuffner
'*Schwanengesang*' (Swansong) — series of songs —
    seven by Rellstab:
    Liebesbotschaft (Love's Message)
    Kriegers Ahnung (Warrior's Foreboding)
    Frühlingssehnsucht (Longing for Spring)
    Ständchen (Serenade)
    Aufenthalt (Resting Place)
    In der Ferne (In the Distance)
    Abschied (Farewell)

and seven by Heine:

    Der Atlas (Atlas)
    Ihr Bild (Her Portrait)
    Das Fischermädchen (The Fishergirl)
    Die Stadt (The Town)
    Am Meer (By the Sea)
    Der Doppelgänger (The Double)

September
Sonatas in C minor, A major, B flat major.
String Quintet in C major (for 2 violins, viola, 2 cellos)

October
Alternative Benedictus for Mass No. 4 in C major
Tantum Ergo in E flat
Offertory in B flat, Intende Voci
Hymne an den Heiligen Geist (Schmidl), this time for double male voice chorus, soloist and chorus and orchestra
Der Taubenpost (The Pigeon Post)
Der Hirt auf dem Felsen (The Shepherd on the Rocks) by Müller and von Chezy for mezzo-soprano solo with clarinet and pianoforte accompaniment

The Mass and the other liturgical works to which he devoted June, July and his last working month, October, show that Schubert was hoping to establish himself as a liturgical composer in order to secure the lucrative patronage of the church. He needed a regular income, and all other means had failed him. He must have realized that a position as a *Kapellmeister*, so often held by composers, was the only course left to him. His financial situation, despite the success of his concert, was worse, and so was his health. His friends, so many now married and all with safe professions, were in direct contrast to his own insecure 'bohemian' existence. So Schubert devoted his precious time and creative energy to a series of works which are all well below the level of his best compositions; indeed, writing liturgical music seemed to bring out the worst in him. It is sad he should have spent so much of his last month on a lengthy Offertory, *Intende Voci*, for tenor solo chorus and orchestra, and two other liturgical works. The only songs he wrote during that

month were the delightful *Taubenpost* and the ambitious, lengthy *Der Hirt auf dem Felsen*, specially written for his old friend the singer Anna Milder-Hauptmann who wanted a virtuoso piece and was given one: the song is a joyful coloratura rapture at the return of spring with the shepherd's piping represented by a clarinet obligato. Also during October he made arrangements to take lessons in fugue and counterpoint from a contemporary of his, Simon Sechter, as part of his campaign to master the required liturgical style, so foreign to his natural creative impulse. Schubert's knowledge of counterpoint was in fact profound; but the writing of church music was a specialized business and he clearly felt the need to learn the necessary techniques. His near-pastiche of Handel, *Mirjam's Seigegesang*, was an earlier step on the same road. He had acquired scores of Handel's works late in 1827, and Leopold Sonnleithner recalls Schubert's comment on these: 'Now for the first time I see what I lack'. This remark must be seen in its contemporary context: Beethoven had made Handel the musician's ideal because he had stated that Handel was the greatest composer who had ever lived. 'Handel, to him I bow the knee.'

But neither the Handelian nor the liturgical style drew from Schubert anything more than his second-best inspiration. Perhaps, in the course of time, his return to the study of classical forms might have had exciting effects on his own special idiom, but Schubert was given no more time.

* * *

I have known four musicians, all greatly experienced in this class of music, and none in the least inclined by disposition to sentimentality, who with strange unanimity expressed the feeling that, were they fated in their last hours to listen to some lovely strain, this would be the music of their election.

(W. W. Cobbett 'Cyclopedic Survey of Chamber Music')

The 'lovely strain' is the *Adagio* of Schubert's C major String Quintet; this movement, one of the miracles of music, moves the listener to the depths of the heart. 'I hold the very look on paper of this E major *Adagio* to be beautiful', wrote Richard Capell. Schubert composed his Quintet from the purest creative impulse; there was no commission, no other outside reason why he should have written a Quintet at this particular time. Possibly he wanted to test his own versatility; it had been a year of new departures.

This intensely personal work is the creative and spiritual *summa* of Schubert's life. All he has known during his short, full existence, all the gaiety, the pain, the joy, the anguish, the exalted spiritual understanding, the black melancholy, the innocence, the experience — all these fill the Quintet. In it there is music of

Mozart, Haydn, and Beethoven

George Frideric Handel

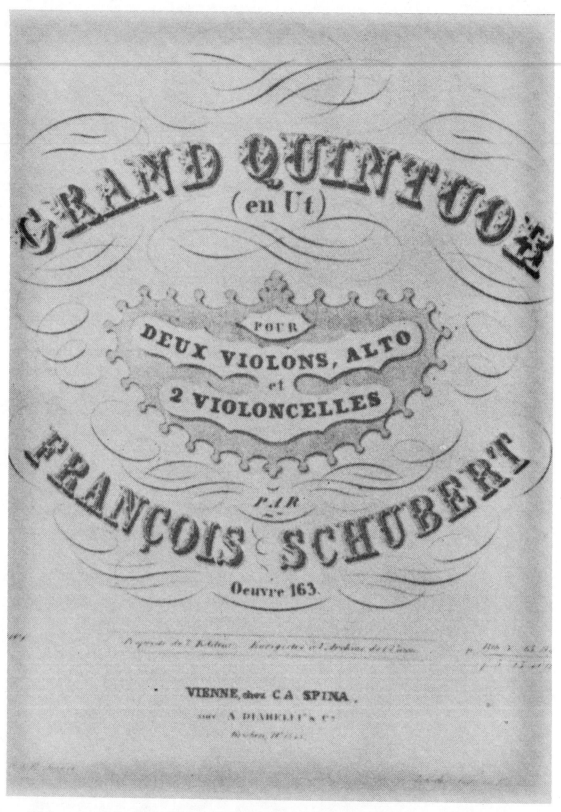

Title page of the first edition of the String Quintet in C (1828)

passionate intensity, of romantic sadness, of ominous turbulence, of joy and feverish gaiety. But there is no serenity: this is the music of an urgent, active man about to enter the prime of his life.

Schubert altered the usual balance of instruments in the quintet: Mozart's accepted pattern was to add a second viola to the basic string quartet, but Schubert instead used a second cello. This gave him important advantages: with a doubly firm bass line he could let one cello soar while the other supported it; and he could combine two or three instruments in extraordinarily rich ways — for instance, in the *adagio* the theme is played by the three 'middle' instruments, second violin, viola and first cello, while the first violin and second cello support and decorate. Finally, the presence of the extra cello gives the whole masterpiece its special dark, rich, warmly sombre and yet luminous sound.

If any answer were needed to those who hold that Schubert's command of form and structure was insecure, it lies in the first movement. Burnett James' description of it could not be bettered:

Out of two main themes of unsurpassed lyric splendour, plus a few derivatives, Schubert builds a movement that is in its way unparalleled in all chamber music for its variety of colour and emotion and technical effectiveness. The development section is built from a figure that is a sort of postlude to the exposition and is wonderfully bound together and crossbraced by exceptionally ingenious devices of counterpoint. In the recapitulation the strains of tender beauty and pathos rise to new imaginative heights through subtle variations of instrumental colour. Here Schubert shows his unique sensitivity, especially when the theme announced in the exposition by the two cellos is given to cello and viola and then passes to a variant on the violins.

Every new hearing of this Quintet reveals fresh riches to the ear and heart; and at each hearing we discover again — sometimes with a sense of shock at the strength of emotional involvement demanded of us — the distillation of everything that Schubert was on earth to tell us.

Chapter 12

Untimely Death

'Schubert's transparent art miraculously preserves the image of his beautiful and unconscious youth. He died, and will never grow old.' — Richard Capell

On the first day of September 1828 Schubert moved out of his comfortable rooms at Schober's to his brother Ferdinand's house in the Neue Wieden suburb. Schubert's health had deteriorated; his fits of giddiness were worse, and his illness appears to have entered a new phase, weakening him generally. His doctor, the court physician Ernst von Rinna, thought the fresh air of the suburb would do him good. Unfortunately Ferdinand's house was newly built and had not dried out yet, and the sanitary arrangements in that as yet rudimentary street were still insufficient. So though there was open air and countryside around, the house itself was worse for Schubert's health than his rooms in the inner city.

Schubert obviously regarded the stay as temporary: he left all his manuscripts behind in the 'music closet' at Schober's. He also still hoped to fit in a short holiday at Graz; Jenger wrote to Marie Pachler on 6 September and said he had been trying to discover Schubert's new whereabouts:

Last night I spoke to him at last at the Burg Theatre, and I am now able to tell you, dear lady, that friend Schwammerl [Tubby] expects an improvement in his finances shortly, and confidently reckons, as soon as this has happened, to avail himself immediately of your kind invitation, . . .

But by the end of September Schubert wrote despondently to Jenger that the trip to Graz was off 'as money and weather are wholly unfavourable'. On 2nd October, he despatched letters to both his new publishers, Schott's in Mainz and Probst in Leipzig; the latter is, as O. E. Deutsch says, 'like a cry of distress'.

Sir,

I beg to inquire when at last the Trio is to appear. Can it be that you do not know the opus number yet? It is Op. 100. I await its appearance with longing. I have composed, among other things, 3 sonatas for pianoforte solo, which I should like to dedicate to Hummel. Moreover, I have set several songs by Heine of Hamburg, which pleased extraordinarily here, and finally turned out a Quintet for 2 violins, 1 viola and 2 violoncellos. The sonatas I have played with much success in several places, but the Quintet will be tried out only during the coming days. [The Quintet was finally published in 1853; the first public performance was in 1850.]

Schubert is offering Probst, who had behaved badly over the Trio, all his latest and best works; he had in fact planned to publish the Heine songs as a cycle dedicated to his friends, but clearly financial pressure has made him sacrifice this idea.

The Rellstab and Heine songs were published after Schubert's death as a cycle, named *Schwanengesang* by the publisher. They are a group, a series, not a cycle as *Winterreise* is; the Rellstab songs are beautiful, assured and attractive, but the seven poems by Heinrich Heine drew superlative music from Schubert. Each poem sparely and vividly isolates and crystallizes a human emotion: in *Der Atlas*, the exalted despair that can come to the heart when it has had the courage to be fully vulnerable; in *Der Doppelgänger*, the nostalgic bitterness and pain aroused by a place where a man has endured the pangs of unrequited love — in this case the poet thinks he sees his double wringing his hands outside his sweetheart's former house; and in *Die Stadt*, where the emotion expressed is complex and opaque. This poem illustrates to perfection the kind of poetry which most inspired Schubert, with its sharply suggested landscape, and the credible human emotion of the poet identifying

The house of Ferdinand Schubert, where the composer died

himself with this landscape and receiving from it, as the sun pierces the mist and illuminates the town, an equally illuminating moment of self-knowledge.

On the distant horizon
like a misty image appears
the town with its turrets
veiled in evening twilight.

A damp gust ruffles
the grey expanse of water;
with weary strokes
the boatman rows my boat.

The sun rises once again,
radiant, from the earth,
and shows me the place
where I loved and lost.

The gusts ruffling the grey water, the tired rowing, the shaft of sunlight — all these are magically captured by Schubert's music. It is the small circumstantial detail he transforms and makes not only unforgettable, but permanently significant: the hat blowing off, the bee brushing the lute strings, waves rocking a boat at night, the fisherman coldly watching the beautiful and playful trout. The way he captures these details in music shows how completely Schubert was part of the Romantic imagination of his period; Coleridge's words defining his and Wordsworth's aims in that seminal Romantic work, *The Lyrical Ballads* (first published in 1798) also sum up this aspect of Schubert's achievement:

to give the charm of novelty to things of every day, and to excite a feeling analogous to the supernatural, by awakening the mind's attention from the lethargy of custom, and directing it to the loveliness and the wonders of the world before us; an inexhaustible treasure, but for which in consequence of the film of familiarity and selfish solicitude we have eyes, yet see not, ears that hear not, and hearts that neither feel nor understand . . .

For the Romantics, Nature was a powerful factor in man's destiny; reflecting and affecting his passions, and illuminating their significance. Poems on this theme inspired a large proportion of Schubert's greatest songs; *Die Stadt* is one of the purest.

Early in October, after writing his despairing letter to Probst, Schubert set out on a walking tour with his brother Ferdinand and two friends. His health had continued to deteriorate and a short holiday consisting of exercise and fresh air seemed a good idea. Ferdinand describes how they made 'a little pleasure trip to Unter-Waltersdorf, and thence an excursion to Eisenstadt, where he

[Schubert] sought out Josef Haydn's tomb and remained at its side for a fairly long time. He ate and drank most modestly during these three days of travel, but was very bright withal and had many merry notions. But once he was back in Vienna, his indisposition increased once more.'

Many biographers assume that this exercise was bad for Schubert, weakened and slightly overweight as he was, and helped to bring about his end. But on 3 November, clearly feeling the need of it, he took another long walk with Ferdinand and thus it seems more likely that far from having a debilitating effect, these walks gave Schubert pleasure and strength in his last weeks.

Another heartening pleasure must have been the letter he received from his friend Anton Schindler, temporarily in Budapest, urging him to go there and give a concert of his songs. A clear picture of Schubert's nature emerges from Schindler's remarks and affectionate criticism. Schindler says the success of a concert would be assured, and urges Schubert, despite 'your timidity and easy-going ways', to procure himself some letters of introduction from noble houses like Count Esterhàzy's:

Do not let this be a burden to you, for it will involve no trouble and no wire-pulling, but simply deliver the letters here, if we regard it as expedient, and with that *basta*! To get a few hundred florins into your pocket in this manner is a thing not to be despised, and apart from that other advantages may accrue therefrom. To it, then! Do not argue for long, and make no bones about it! You will be well and energetically supported. There is a young dilettante here who sings your songs with a fine tenor voice well, really quite well, and he is with us; the gentlemen of the theatre ditto, my sister ditto; in this way you need only deposit your fat carcass here and accompany whatever is performed. Songs for several voices cannot fail to make their effect either. Some of them are known here. Write nothing new: it is not necessary!

Of course Schubert could not even consider a trip to Budapest: his health was bad, and the journey would have taken 28 hours. And now, on top of his chronic condition, a new infection invaded him. Ferdinand describes how the symptoms began:

Then on the last day of October, when he wished to eat some fish in the evening, he suddenly threw his knife and fork on the plate as soon as he had tasted the first morsel, suggesting that he found his food immensely repellent and felt just as though he had taken poison. From that moment Schubert hardly ate or drank anything more, taking nothing but medicines. He also tried to find relief by moving in the fresh air, and therefore still took a few walks.

In fact, after this first onset of nausea, Schubert appears to have

151

continued his life more or less as normal for the next week or so. Some time during his last weeks he heard (and, it appears, played the viola part in) Beethoven's C minor Quartet, Opus 131. It is said Schubert 'was sent into such transports of delight and enthusiasm that all feared for him'. He is also reported to have been to Baron Schönstein's one evening where 'he was very cheerful, indeed almost unrestrained in his gaiety'.

Schubert's feverish gaiety fits into the pattern of the dreadful disease he now had: typhoid fever. It follows a three-week course: the first week the patient seems fairly normal but suffers sickness, headaches and extremes of mood; the second week shows a rapid deterioration and in the third week delirium develops followed by death.

Ferdinand tells us that Schubert took to his bed on 14 November, but it was probably a couple of days before that, because on 12 November Schubert wrote a letter to Schober, the last letter he ever wrote:

Dear Schober,
    I am ill. I have eaten nothing for eleven days and drunk nothing, and I totter feebly and shakily from my chair to bed and back again.
    Rinna is treating me. If ever I take anything, I bring it up again at once.
    Be so kind, then, as to assist me in this desperate situation by means of literature. Of Cooper's I have read 'The Last of the Mohicans', 'The Spy', 'The Pilot' and 'The Pioneers'. If by any chance you have anything else of his, I implore you to deposit it with Frau von Bogner at the coffee-house for me. My brother, who is conscientiousness itself, will most faithfully pass it on to me. Or anything else.
                    Your friend
                    Schubert.

The second stage of the disease had begun; Schubert sounds stunned by the strength of the fever and nausea he is experiencing. Fennimore Cooper's books were very popular in Austria and Germany, and were translated the moment a new one was written; Schober sent the books, but did not visit Schubert himself. He was accustomed to the composer's illness, and perhaps did not realize the gravity of the last development until too late. As Bauernfeld put it: 'But who believes in sickness and in death when they are young?'

On 16 November two new doctors, von Vering (an expert on syphilitic disorders) and Wisgrill took over from Rinna who had fallen ill himself. Schubert's treatment was changed, presumably because typhoid fever had now been diagnosed. Schubert was lovingly and carefully nursed not only by his family — by Ferdinand and Anna his wife, and by Josepha, Schubert's thirteen-year-old stepsister — but also by two paid nurses, a male and a female.

Franz Lachner at the graves of Schubert and Beethoven (*drawing by Schwind*)

Schubert took his medicines punctually; his watch hung on a chair by his bed. His room was small, with a window on the street.

Spaun visited his old friend, taking some music (a copy of *Ständchen*) for him to look through.

I found him ill in bed, though his condition did not seem to me at all serious. He corrected my copy in bed, was glad to see me and said, 'There is really nothing the matter with me, only I am so exhausted I feel as if I were going to fall through the bed'. He was cared for most affectionately by a charming 13-year-old sister, whom he praised very highly to me. I left him without any anxiety at all, and it came as a thunderbolt when, a few days later, I heard of his death.

Bauernfeld and Lachner visited Schubert on 17 November; Lachner was about to leave Vienna on business.

Anxiety concerning Schubert's condition, who had been completely bed-ridden since 10 November, made the parting difficult for me. He had been ailing ever since he had gone to live with his brother, Ferdinand, in the newly built house in the Lumpertgasse (now Kettenbrückengasse 6) before the onset of winter (end of September). When I came into his room he was lying with his face turned to the wall in the deepest feverish delirium. Added to this were scanty nursing and a badly heated room, on the walls of which the damp was running down! During a lucid moment I took my leave of him and told him I hoped to be back in four days. But when I returned to Vienna on 21 November Schubert was already in his grave.

153

This memory was written down long after the event, and there is no doubt Lachner is wrong about the scanty nursing, though perhaps not about the lack of warmth and the damp.

Bauernfeld's description feels a closer one to reality; he implies it was the letter to Schober which sent him hurrying round to his friend's bedside. He seems to have paid more than one visit.

When I went to see Schubert for the last time — it was on 17 November — he was in a very bad way and complained of weakness and burning in his head; but in the afternoon he was still perfectly clear and without any sign of delirum, although the depressed mood of my friend filled me with evil forebodings. — His brother came with the doctors — already by evening the invalid was raving violently and he never regained consciousness — the most severe typhoid fever had set in.

But it was Schubert's close family who had to bear the strain of his tragic end. He became violently delirious on the night of 17 November, and the next day it was difficult to restrain him. Schubert's old father wrote to comfort Ferdinand:

My dear son Ferdinand,
    Days of gloom and sorrow weigh heavily upon us. The dangerous illness of our beloved Franz acts painfully on our spirits. Nothing remains for us in these sad days except to seek comfort in God . . . See to it, to the best of your ability, that our good Franz is forthwith provided with the Holy Sacraments for the dying, and I shall live in the comforting hope that God will fortify and keep him.

This marble monument by Karl Kundmann (1872) now stands in the Vienna City Park

Schubert was not conscious enough to take communion; he simply received extreme unction. Ferdinand described the last hours in a letter written to his father two days after Schubert's death:

For on the evening before his death, though only half conscious, he still said to me: 'I implore you to transfer me to my room, not to leave me here, in this corner under the earth; do I then deserve no place above the earth?' I answered him: 'Dear Franz, rest assured, believe your brother Ferdinand, whom you have always trusted, and who loves you so much. You are in the room in which you have always been so far, and lie in your bed!' — And Franz said: 'No, it is not true: Beethoven does not lie here.' — Could this be anything but an indication of his inmost wish to repose by the side of Beethoven, whom he so greatly revered . . .

Schubert kept trying to get out of bed, imagining in his delirium he was in some strange room. Ferdinand did his best to quieten and reassure him.

A few hours later the doctor appeared, who persuaded him in similar words. But Schubert looked fixedly into the doctor's eyes, grasped at the

In 1863 the bodies of Beethoven and Schubert were exhumed and re-buried in metal coffins. In 1888 they found their final resting place in the Musicians' Grove of the newly-laid-out Central Cemetery of Vienna. Monuments (from left to right) of Beethoven, Mozart and Schubert

wall with a feeble hand, and said slowly and seriously: 'Here, here is my end!'

Schubert died at 3 o'clock in the afternoon of 19 November, aged not quite thirty-two.

'I have wept for him as for a brother', wrote Schwind to Schober when he heard while in Munich of his beloved friend's death.

I have wept for him as for a brother, but now I am glad for him that he has died in his greatness and has done with his sorrows. The more I realize now what he was like, the more I see what he has suffered . . . The recollection of him will be with us, and all the burdens of the world will not prevent us now and again from feeling most deeply what has now utterly vanished.

Bauernfeld wrote, stunned, in his diary:

Yesterday afternoon Schubert died. On Monday I still spoke to him. On Tuesday he was delirious, on Wednesday dead. To the last he talked to me of our opera. It all seems like a dream to me.

Spaun's cry is for us all:

Poor Schubert, so young and at the start of such a brilliant career! What a wealth of untapped treasures his death has robbed us of!

155

Memorial bust by
Joseph Dialer
(*Historische Museum,
Vienna*)

On 21 November, Schubert was buried next to Beethoven in the new Währing Cemetery, after a service in St Joseph's Church. His funeral was a moderately elaborate one, a great expense for Ferdinand and old Franz: 'Much! Very much! Yet surely very little for Franz! . . .' The illness had been very expensive for them all too, but Ferdinand adds reassuringly:

I think we may expect with certainty that all the expenses caused by his illness and his burial etc., will soon be defrayed by what he has left . . .

So Schubert was buried with fitting honours in a painted coffin with a 'fine shroud', and a 'handsome cross' and a 'handsome pall' were provided for the man to whom religious rites meant so little. Schober was asked by the family to write a special poem to be sung at the funeral; he composed it in the metre of his *Pax Vobiscum* set by Schubert in 1817. The poem, alas rather unimpressive, ends

> So let us ever follow each sweet note
> That we may meet again in worlds remote.

Many people came to the funeral despite the bad weather.

Then it was over, and all that Schubert had left behind him was sorted and listed; the few possessions of a careless bachelor were described in the official document:

3 cloth coats, 3 frock coats, 10 pairs of trousers, 9 waistcoats

1 hat, 5 pairs of shoes, 2 pairs of boots, 4 shirts, 9 neckerchiefs and pocket handkerchiefs

13 pairs of socks, 1 sheet, 2 blankets,
1 mattress, 1 featherbed cover, 1 counterpane.

Apart from some old music . . . no belongings of the deceased are to be found.

But in the music closet in the Tuchlauben, and scattered in his friends' possession all over Austria, were the manuscripts of Schubert's music, that incomparable collection whose worth was beyond any gold.

* * *

> I am Schubert! Franz Schubert!
> And don't you forget it!

INDEX

Selected listing of references
Illustrations are indicated in bold type

ILLUSTRATIONS ADDED FOR EXPANDED EDITION

In creating this expanded edition, about forty illustrations have been added as unnumbered pages at various places within the text. Following is a key to those insertions.